Endorsements

"This is an important book for all Christians interested in bringing their beliefs to bear upon the world around them. Abortion is one of the most critical issues of our day, and R. C. Sproul looks at it through the lenses of theology, philosophy, and reason. This book is refreshingly free of hyperbole, and yet does not compromise the truth."

—JIM DALY
President, Focus on the Family
Colorado Springs, Colorado

"R. C. Sproul's rapier logic will put to flight rationalistic defenders of abortion. Those torn between conflicting claims about the humanity of the unborn, the role of government, and the rights of women will find this book particularly instructive."

—MARVIN OLASKY
Editor-in-chief, WORLD magazine
Provost, The King's College
New York City

"When I read R. C. Sproul's book on abortion twenty years ago, I was still a pastor. I recall how grateful I was that a respected theologian had spoken out so clearly on the critical issue of abortion. At the time, such voices were few and far between, with many evangelical theologians seemingly silent about the plight of unborn children. Sproul's logic is sharp and penetrating, and his reliance on biblical authority is refreshing. The appendix, in which Dr. Jerome Lejeune offers courtroom testimony, is a great bonus. I'm happy to recommend the re-release of Dr. Sproul's book on this vital subject, and I pray God will use it to enlighten many new readers."

—RANDY ALCORN
Founder and director, Eternal Perspective Ministries
Sandy, Oregon
Author of *ProLife Answers to ProChoice Arguments* and *Why Prolife?*

"R. C. Sproul's book on abortion is a classic text in the evangelical witness against the culture of death. I pray this Twentieth Anniversary Edition will awaken a new generation of Christians to the joyful duty of protecting the 'least of these,' our Lord Jesus' unborn brothers and sisters."

—RUSSELL D. MOORE
Dean, School of Theology
The Southern Baptist Theological Seminary
Louisville, Kentucky

"R. C. Sproul covers the issues candidly and objectively—without the emotion and demagoguery that so often pervade the abortion debate. You are the jury; you decide the verdict."

—JOHN MACARTHUR
Pastor-teacher, Grace Community Church
Sun Valley, California

"Staying silent on the issue of abortion is no longer an option. It is time for those who are respected and capable to speak out and say it straight. I know of no one who qualifies better than R. C. Sproul."

—Chuck Swindoll
Senior pastor, Stonebriar Community Church
Frisco, Texas

"Classic Sproul! Logical, clear, fair, attempting to understand the pro-choice views while all the time making a solid, biblical pro-life apologetic that seeks both to convince the opponents but also to bring about in practical ways the end of this North American holocaust. Add to that the foreword of George Grant and you have a winner."

—Peter Jones
Executive director, truthXchange
Escondido, California

"I am delighted to see this Twentieth Anniversary Edition of *Abortion: A Rational Look at an Emotional Issue*. It was and continues to be an important contribution to the pro-life movement and to the defense of the sanctity of human life."

—John Jefferson Davis
Professor of systematic theology and Christian ethics
Gordon-Conwell Theological Seminary
South Hamilton, Massachusetts

twentieth anniversary edition

abortion

// a rational look at an emotional issue

R.C. SPROUL

R

Reformation Trust
PUBLISHING

A DIVISION OF LIGONIER MINISTRIES · ORLANDO, FLORIDA

Abortion: A Rational Look at an Emotional Issue

© 1990, 2010 by R.C. Sproul

Previously published (1990) by NavPress.

Published by Reformation Trust Publishing
a division of Ligonier Ministries
400 Technology Park, Lake Mary, FL 32746
www.ligonier.org   www.reformationtrust.com

Printed in Harrisonburg, Virginia
RR Donnelley and Sons
March 2011
Second edition, second printing

Cover design: Gearbox Studios
Interior design and typeset: Katherine Lloyd, The DESK

Library of Congress Cataloging-in-Publication Data

Sproul, R.C. (Robert Charles), 1939-
   Abortion : a rational look at an emotional issue / R.C. Sproul. -- 20th anniversary
ed.
      p. cm.
   "Previously published (1990) by NavPress. Second edition 2010"--T.p. verso.
   Includes bibliographical references and index.
   ISBN 978-1-56769-209-9
   1. Abortion--Moral and ethical aspects. 2. Abortion--Religious aspects--Christi-
anity.
   3. Pro-life movement--United States. I. Title.
   HQ767.15.S67 2010
   363.46--dc22
                        2010017013

to Andrea Krazeise

for her heroism in ministry to pregnant women in crisis

Contents

PART I: ABORTION: THE ETHICAL DILEMMA
OF OUR TIME

PART II: AN ANALYSIS OF PRO-ABORTION
AND PRO-CHOICE ARGUMENTS

PART III: A COMPASSIONATE RESPONSE AND STRATEGY

Foreword

In the two decades since this landmark book was first published, four different presidents have occupied the White House, seven justices have come and gone on the Supreme Court, and eleven sessions of Congress have held sway in the Capitol.

These federal magistrates have faced economic booms and busts. They have weathered terror attacks and foreign wars. They have witnessed the end of the Cold War and the rise of the al Qaeda menace. They have wrangled over corporate bailouts and health-care reforms. They have endured Tea Party protests, campaign scandals, personal embarrassments, and policy failures. They have been plagued on every side by mounting demands, frustrated expectations, declining resources, and diminished prestige.

Through it all, the divisiveness of the abortion issue has remained constant. The many and varied political turns of events during the past twenty years have done nothing to ameliorate it—much less, to resolve it. If anything, the divide over abortion has become more pronounced, more acrimonious, and more entrenched. While political gridlock on nearly any and every other issue ultimately has been overcome, no rapprochement on the issue of abortion is anywhere in sight.

Of course, matters have not exactly been helped by the fact

that the politically protected international abortion business has grown into a multibillion-dollar industrial complex. Utilizing its considerable wealth, manpower, and influence, the abortion industry has proven itself adept at muscling its way into virtually every facet of modern life.[1] It now plays a strategic role in the health and social-services community.[2] It exerts a major influence on education, providing the majority of sex-education curricula and programs in both public and private schools.[3] It carries considerable political clout through lobbying, campaigning, advocacy, and litigation.[4] It is involved in publishing, broadcast media production, judicial activism, public relations, foreign aid, psychological research counseling, environmental policy-making, sociological planning, demographic investigation, pharmacological development, contraceptive distribution and sales, mass advertising, and public legal service provision.[5]

Planned Parenthood, the oldest, largest, and best-organized provider of abortion and birth-control services in the world, has become a tenured player in all the great social and political issues of our day.[6] From its ignoble beginnings around the turn of the twentieth century, when the shoestring operation consisted of an illegal back-alley clinic in a shabby Brooklyn neighborhood, staffed by a shadowy clutch of firebrand activists and anarchists,[7] it has expanded dramatically into a conglomerate with programs and activities in 134 nations and on every continent.[8]

In the United States alone, Planned Parenthood has mobilized more than twenty thousand personnel and volunteers along the front lines of the confrontational and vitriolic battle over abortion. Today those minions man the organization's more than 150 affiliates and its nearly one thousand clinics in virtually every major metropolitan area, coast to coast.[9] It boasts a national headquarters in New York, a legislative center in Washington, regional command posts in Atlanta, Chicago, Miami, and San Francisco, affiliate offices in 49 states and the District of Columbia, and international centers in London, Nairobi, Bangkok, and New Delhi. With an estimated combined annual budget—including all its regional, national, and international service affiliates—of more than a billion dollars, this leading light of the abortion industry may well be the largest and most profitable nonprofit organization in history.[10]

As if that were not enough, the current Democratic administration in Washington—aided and abetted by the Democrat-controlled Senate and House of Representatives—is the most ardently pro-abortion in American history.[11] With a bevy of executive orders, appointments, and administrative policy changes—to say nothing of its 2,407-page monolithic, partisan "health-care-reform" legislation, which removed the longstanding ban on federal funding of abortions in favor of a much more easily overturned executive order—the abortion industry has logged more gains during this administration's short tenure than in the rest of its history combined.[12]

Yet the great divide persists. Despite its obvious cultural clout, its cavernously deep corporate pockets, and its carefully crafted public-relations efforts, the abortion industry has yet to prevail in the battle for the hearts and minds of most Americans. Public-opinion polls conducted during the first year of the

Obama administration found that 51 percent of Americans now call themselves "pro-life" on the issue of abortion, while only 42 percent call themselves "pro-choice."[13] In addition, the number of Americans who favor making it more difficult to obtain an abortion is up six percentage points in just five years. In 2005, 59 percent of respondents agreed it would be good to reduce abortions. Today, 65 percent take this view. One poll also found that fewer Americans, and fewer pro-life activists, are willing to compromise on abortion by finding some "middle ground." Indeed, support for finding a middle ground on the abortion issue is down twelve percentage points among conservatives and six points among all Americans.[14] Yet another poll found that 58 percent of Americans say abortion is morally wrong most of the time. Just 25 percent disagree, and the rest have no opinion. The poll found women are more strongly pro-life than men, with 64 percent of women asserting that most abortions are morally wrong, a view shared by 51 percent of men. Meanwhile, still another survey found a majority of Americans, 52 percent, think it is too easy to get an abortion in America. That's up seven percentage points from two years ago, when 45 percent thought it was too easy.[15]

So why does it seem that the abortion Goliath's grassroots support is slipping at the very moment when its power and resources have reached their zenith? At least part of the reason may be the very nature of the abortion business itself—along with the inevitable fallout that accompanies it. Consider:

• Although heralded by the abortion lobby as both "safe and legal," it is now apparent that abortion is merely "legal." The complications of this, the most commonly performed medical procedure in America today, are legion. They include sterility—occurring in as many as 25 percent of all women receiving mid-trimester abortions; hemorrhaging—nearly 10 percent of all cases require transfusions; viral hepatitis—occurring in 10 percent of all those transfused; embolism—occurring in as many as 4 percent of all cases; cervical laceration; pelvic inflammatory disease; genital tract infection; cardiorespiratory arrest; acute kidney failure; and amniotic fluid embolus.[16]

• As a result of these sundry complications, women in America have seen a massive increase in the cost of medical care. While the average cost of normal health maintenance for men has increased nearly 12 percent over the past fifteen years due to inflation, the average cost for women has skyrocketed a full 27 percent.[17]

• A spate of medical malpractice lawsuits from botched abortions has intensified the industry's already looming insurability crisis.[18]

• At the same time, the cultural and political stigmatization of abortion providers has dramatically reduced the number of qualified physicians willing to serve them. As a result, many clinics have been forced to rely on less adequately trained personnel—nurse practitioners and doctors who more often than not have failed in private or institutional practices.[19]

• Revelations about deliberately suppressed research data on various procedural risks—particularly concerning the established links between abortion and breast cancer—have raised new questions about the industry's medical objectivity and professional integrity.[20]

• New clinical evidence exposing the grave hazards of several of the other forms of treatment championed by the industry—from the deleterious effects of the RU-486 abortion drug and the Norplant contraceptive surgery to the inherent risks and complications in the use of intrauterine devices—have raised the specter of "wholesale institutional quackery."[21]

• The shadow over the industry's iatrogenic carelessness has been further darkened by its enthusiastic defense of the horrifying second-trimester "dilation and extraction" surgical procedure—commonly known as D&X or "partial-birth" abortion.[22]

• In addition, the industry has staked its tenuous reputation on the therapeutic usefulness of two very dangerous new chemical treatments—the Depo-Provera long-term contraceptive injection and the Methotrexate-Misoprostol abortifacient. Both drugs present grave hazards to women's health, according to a battery of recent clinical tests.[23]

• Horrifying new evidence of barbaric human-rights violations—including forced abortions, coercive sterilizations, and torturous disfigurement—associated with the Planned Parenthood-designed population program in Communist China has cast an ominous shadow over the industry's innumerable other tax-funded international activities.[24]

• Not surprisingly, the bridling of information about viable alternatives to the abortion industry's clinical, educational, and surgical services has provoked the wrath of a variety of health-care consumer advocates.[25]

• Parents, outraged at the promiscuity-promoting content of the abortion industry's affiliated sex-education materials,

AIDS-awareness programs, and community-advocacy projects, have begun to organize grassroots efforts to bar organizations such as Planned Parenthood from schools, charitable networks, and civic coalitions in communities all across the United States.[26]

• Several punitive lawsuits initiated by the abortion industry—filed in an effort to close down pro-life adoption agencies and abortion-alternative crisis pregnancy centers—have begun to reinforce a perception that the organization is more concerned with the ideological enforcement of its agenda than with the health and welfare of its clients.[27]

• A series of negative public-relations campaigns launched by the well-heeled abortion lobby—against cultural conservatives in general and Christian conservatives in particular—has highlighted the industry's immoderate aims and set the standard for the increasingly shrill rhetoric and hysterical extremism of the pro-abortion movement.[28]

• Conflict-of-interest accusations have begun to circulate in Washington concerning the cozy relationships between certain past and present federal officials and the industry's voluble lobbyists on Capitol Hill.[29]

• A backlash against the massively unpopular "health-care-reform" legislation passed in early 2010 not only has brought renewed support for pro-life organizations, crisis pregnancy centers, and principled politicians, it has brought renewed scrutiny to the grisly abortion trade. New calls to enforce existing laws and enact stricter new ones bode ill for the industry's plans for growth and expansion.[30]

In short, one scandal after another has hit the abortion industry, its medical personnel, its educators, its researchers, its lobbyists, and its administrators. As a result, its "Teflon" reputation is starting to wear a little thin and its "grand illusion" has begun to lose its luster.[31]

As a result, Dr. Sproul's incisive analysis in this book is as relevant and necessary today as it was in the last decade of the twentieth century. Indeed, he points the way to the only possible resolution of this deeply emotional issue.

Once before in American history, a national pro-life consensus was forged, laws were changed, and life was protected. At the outset of the nineteenth century, abortion was actually legal—if only marginally—in every state in the Union. By the end of the century, the procedure had been universally criminalized.

Most of the legal changes came during a relatively short twenty-year period, from 1860 to 1880.[32] In less than two decades, Christians were able to recruit hostile journalists, ambivalent physicians, reticent politicians, and even radical feminists to the cause of mothers with crisis pregnancies and their unborn children. They succeeded overwhelmingly despite the vast wealth, power, and political clout of the burgeoning abortion industry. At a time when the nation was riven with strife over the recalcitrance of chattel slavery, the proliferation of abortion, and the challenging of the most basic principles of American liberty, they demonstrated in word and deed that every human being is made in the image of God and is thus sacred.

The popular press made information about abortion available to the average man on the street. The medical associations made physicians aware of the physical risks and the moral compromises inherently involved in the procedure. Lawyers, politicians, and judges enacted the legal constraints necessary to criminalize abortion profiteers. But it was the church that catalyzed and spearheaded the wildly successful pro-life efforts of the nineteenth century.[33]

It is probably not surprising that pro-life stalwarts of nineteenth-century America did not simply say "no" to abortion; they said "yes" to women in crisis. They said "yes" to the poor and desperate. They said "yes" to the confused and afflicted. In short, they fulfilled their servanthood mandate simultaneously with their prophetic mandate.

Lives were saved, families restored, and the men and women who dedicated themselves to the cause of the sanctity of human life laid a remarkable foundation of liberty for future generations. America at last seemed poised to fulfill her promise—as the land of the free and the home of the brave.

May it be so yet again. And may God be pleased to use this book as a means to bring to pass this, the church's great work of standing for truth, justice, and mercy in the midst of a poor, fallen world.

—*George Grant*
Franklin, Tennessee
January 2010

Preface

Abortion is an ethical issue, perhaps the central ethical issue of the twentieth and now the twenty-first centuries. As a question of ethics, abortion is not morally neutral; it does not fall within the gray zone of things that are indifferent. There is widespread disagreement about whether abortion on demand is right or wrong, but it cannot be both.

In this book, I seek to examine the ethical implications of abortion. I look at the issue from the perspectives of biblical law, natural law, and positive judicial law.

Although in the pages that follow I will examine arguments from both sides of the debate, I am convinced that abortion on demand is evil. I will try to show that abortion is against the law of God, against the laws of nature, and against reason.

This is intended to be a brief case against abortion. The reader who wrestles with this issue will receive an overview so that he or she may respond to the issue objectively.

To assist the comprehension and use of the book's information, summaries and discussion questions appear at the end of each chapter. Also, the back matter includes a list of agencies offering more information on pro-life groups and adoption, as well as a bibliography and index.

At times, I have used generic terms for human beings, such as *humanity* or *mankind*, for stylistic brevity and to avoid the repetition of "he" and "she." In doing this, it is not my desire to offend any who may be sensitive to the issue of gender in speech. This is especially critical when discussing issues that have been linked so strongly to the broader ethical concerns of the feminist movement. I think it is imperative to distinguish the abortion issue from the feminist issue. However, because concern for women is closely related to the abortion debate, feminism and abortion cannot be totally separated. For clarity's sake, though, they must be distinguished.

My thanks for help in this book go to Maureen Buchman, Gwen Weber, my wife, Vesta, and my son, R.C. I am also grateful to George Grant for his exceptionally helpful foreword for this edition and for helping update the book in light of changes over the past twenty years.

Part I

ABORTION:
THE ETHICAL DILEMMA
OF OUR TIME

Chapter One

A Nation Divided

*Never, never will we desist till we . . . extinguish every
trace of this bloody traffic [slavery], of which our posterity,
looking back to the history of those enlightened times,
will scarce believe that it has been suffered to exist so long
a disgrace and dishonor to this country.*
—William Wilberforce,
1791 speech, House of Commons

A single issue rarely divides the American people. The few that
have include slavery, the civil-rights movement, and the war
in Vietnam. Yet another such issue is roiling in the present, an
issue of such magnitude that our national solidarity is threatened. To many citizens, it is a matter of life and death, and may
be the most serious ethical dilemma ever faced by the United
States. The issue is abortion.

Why should abortion—a matter that many believe should
concern only a woman and her physician—have the potential to rip
apart the social fabric of one of history's most successful nations?

Abortion provokes volatile feelings in combatants on both sides of the debate, which is carried on with heated emotion and militancy. Activists for and against abortion have indulged in strident and inflammatory rhetoric, threatening protests, and even, on occasion, violence, from vandalism to arson and murder. Politicians feel the heat. The abortion issue has become so critical that no candidate for public office can remain silent on his or her views. The politician who tentatively puts his finger to the wind, hoping to gauge the direction of public opinion on abortion, is frustrated by the ever-changing currents. Both sides keep an anxious eye on the health of the current justices of the United States Supreme Court, as the balance of power there is fragile. The addition of one anti-abortion justice to the nation's highest court could precipitate a reversal of the landmark *Roe v. Wade* decision, the 1973 case that made abortion on demand a reality in the United States.

The abortion issue is not only volatile but complex, for it is directly connected to other issues and related popular movements. One example is the feminist movement. Women, who have struggled for decades to secure equal rights under the law and equitable treatment in the business world, fear that a reversal of the abortion laws would signal a serious loss of the gains they have achieved.

Abortion also has been linked to the sexual revolution that swept the country during the 1960s. People who believe that mutually consenting adults have the right to freedom of sexual expression are threatened by the possibility of laws that would invade the "privacy of the bedroom."

The issue of the separation of church and state also looms in the abortion conflict. People on both sides of the debate fear a loss of constitutional rights as a consequence of abortion law. The same constitutional amendment that prohibits the establishment of religion by the state also guarantees the free exercise of religion. There is no question that many, if not the majority, of those who oppose abortion are driven by religious convictions. Religious institutions—including the Roman Catholic Church and many Protestant churches—have taken and continue to take strong stands in opposition to abortion. Those people without church affiliation and those who are affiliated with churches that do not record an anti-abortion stance fear an intrusion into the social and political milieu by the church. They fear a tyranny of religion.

Still others see connections between abortion and a bevy of other issues: education, health-care reform, climate change, social welfare, economic development, government regulation, and foreign aid. Some would even link the abortion issue to the fundamental constitutional right to life, which transcends religious, political, or social considerations. Do the unborn have basic rights that should be protected by constitutional law?

A further issue complicates the matter—the right to freedom of choice, which many Americans consider the most fundamental democratic right of all. Perhaps the most frequently stated sentiment of those caught in the middle of the abortion debate is this: "I would not choose to have an abortion myself, but I would not force my view on someone else." The right to one's opinion is a sacred belief in United States tradition.

Thus, abortion is not a single issue with one solitary facet. It is a multifaceted, complex matter that involves a conflict of perceived rights. No matter how the issue of abortion is resolved, someone's rights—or at least perceived rights—will be in jeopardy. Can such a web of interwoven and conflicting issues be untangled?

The core issue

At the heart of the abortion issue rests one overarching question: Is abortion a form of murder? In other words, does abortion involve the willful destruction of a living human person?

Before discussing this question, certain points must be stated firmly and clearly. First, the vast majority of those advocating the pro-abortion and pro-choice positions are not arguing that women's rights or individual freedom of choice carry with them the right to murder. I am convinced that if the most ardent feminists thought that abortion was in fact a type of murder, they would be as ardently opposed to abortion as they are in favor of equal rights for women.

Though there are many who believe an abortion is justified on the grounds that the developing baby is "unwanted," very few of these people would be in favor of destroying the child after it is born. There are far fewer advocates of infanticide than there are of abortion. The reason for this is clear. In the minds of pro-abortion activists, an unborn baby is not a living human person. Once birth occurs, however, a different set of rules applies. Even in the case of the late-term "partial-birth" abortion procedure, or D&X, all but the most hardened pro-abortion activists argue that the child remains nonviable and nonhuman—and therefore the procedure, however grisly, does not rise to the level of murder.

I labor these points to underscore the reality that pro-abortion and pro-choice activists do not ground their position on some kind of claim for an inalienable right to murder. I am convinced that if somehow it could be proven conclusively that the destruction of unborn babies is in fact the willful destruction of living human beings, the debate on abortion would be all but over, and the law of the land would as clearly prohibit abortion as it does all forms of homicide. The abortion debate is not over whether or not murder should be legalized; it is a debate over whether or not abortion is a kind of murder.

Of course, on the other side of the debate stand the pro-life activists. Those who are pro-life are quite logically also anti-abortion. This group is convinced that abortion is actually a form of murder. Most of them recognize that the intent of abortionists is probably not murder, but they adamantly claim that the act of abortion nevertheless takes the life of a human being.

There is something wrong, however, with even using the word *murder* in this discussion. The word itself is highly charged. At times it is used as a virtual synonym for *homicide*. The law, however, distinguishes between types of homicide. There is a difference between voluntary and involuntary homicide. A further category is manslaughter, both voluntary and involuntary. A clear delineation in the levels of the severity of these crimes exists under the law. Punitive measures for "murder one" (or first-degree murder) are greater than for "murder two" (or second-degree murder) and considerably more severe than for cases of involuntary manslaughter. All three of these terms—*murder, homicide,* and *manslaughter*—are used for the killing of human beings. All are deemed to be serious offenses and crimes against humanity, but their gradations indicate that they are not considered to be crimes of equal severity. We rarely use the word *murderer* for someone who has been convicted of involuntary manslaughter.

The emotional connotation accompanying the word *murder* associates the act of killing with what the law refers to as murder one. Murder one incorporates within its definition the idea of premeditation. It involves malice aforethought. Thus, not only the act of killing a human person is in view, but the motive and intent are also important considerations.

Given this understanding of our use of the term *murder,* we must be careful to insist that pro-abortion and pro-choice activists are not necessarily advocating murder. They are not endorsing the premeditated, willful destruction of human beings with malice aforethought. Almost universally, the proponents of abortion act on the conviction that what is being aborted is less than a human being.

Is a fetus a human being?

To state that abortion is not murder in the first degree because the premeditated intent is absent is not to say that it is legitimate. We already have seen that lesser forms of the killing of human beings are grave and serious evils. Why is abortion not included in the same category?

What is a fetus? The question is objective, not subjective. To determine the status of a fetus is not a matter of personal, arbitrary caprice. The fetus is either alive or not alive. The fetus is either human or not human. The fetus is either a person or not a person. What I *think* the fetus is does not determine which of these it actually is. If a fetus is a living person but I do not believe or think that it is a living person, my thoughts have no bearing on what the fetus *actually* is. By merely thinking or believing, I cannot change what is a person into a nonperson, what is living into unliving, or what is human into nonhuman. By the same token, if the fetus is not a living person, then whatever I believe or think cannot change it into a living person.

Before we can determine whether a fetus is a living human person, we must answer this question: When does life begin? At what point in the continuum of human development do we have a living human person? Does life begin at conception? Does it begin at birth? Or does it begin at some point between these poles of progress, such as at quickening or viability? The answer a person chooses to this question often determines his or her position on the abortion issue.

Because the question of the point of origin of human life is so crucial to the abortion debate, I will devote chapter 4 to the subject. However, some foundational questions must be faced at this point.

It is obvious from the abortion controversy that there is widespread disagreement about when life begins. Pro-abortion activists come to radically different conclusions than those of pro-life activists. The two sides tend to use different methods for finding answers on the question of the origin of life.

Many in the anti-abortion camp base their convictions on inferences drawn from the Bible or from decrees pronounced by their churches. This raises an obvious problem. If one group determines its position exclusively from the Bible or church teaching, what is the effect for people who do not embrace the authority of the Bible or of the church? At this point, the issue of religious tyranny, or the illegitimate intrusion of the church into the realm of the state, rises immediately. In other words, who has the right to say what's right and on what grounds?

The national crisis in ethics

Beneath the division in society over abortion is a more foundational problem: How does one determine what is right? The irony of the United States debate on abortion is that it is a battle over "rights" in a nation that is sharply divided over how to determine what is right about anything. Allan Bloom, in his book *The Closing of the American Mind*, chronicled the epidemic rise of moral relativism that reduces ethics to personal preferences rather than to objective norms for what is right and wrong.

A slogan emerged in the 1960s that crystallized the perspective of moral relativism: "Everyone has the right to do his own thing." This slogan is as crass as it is silly. If it were followed by everyone resolutely, society itself would be an impossibility. No one would have any true rights protected, because at any given moment my rights could trample your rights.

In the late 1960s, I experienced firsthand the ethical insanity of everyone doing his or her own thing. I was working as a pastor in a church. A distressed mother came to me, weeping as Monica wept for her wayward son, who became the great theologian Augustine. The woman related to me that her college-age son had renounced the Christian faith and had moved into a college "pad" adorned with psychedelic posters and black lights. The son wanted to do his "thing," namely, drugs and the pleasure of uninhibited sexual liaisons. The mother pleaded with me to talk to her son about the error of his ways.

I told the woman that I would talk to her son if he was willing to speak with me, but I gave her little encouragement. How open would he be to the counsel of a clergyman forced on him by a parent? To my surprise, the boy came to see me. He was overtly hostile. I asked him why he was so angry. He replied, "Because my mother keeps trying to cram religion down my throat." I nodded in sympathy for his obvious frustration with an overbearing mother.

"What's your alternative ethical system to Christianity?" I asked.

"I believe that everyone has the right to do his own thing," he replied.

"Then what's wrong with your mother's cramming religion down your throat?" I asked.

He did not immediately grasp the point of my question. Instead he launched into a lengthy diatribe against the myriad ways his mother was violating his right to do his own thing. Finally, I said: "But what if your mother's thing is to cram religion down people's throats? Just because it's your throat that religion is being crammed down shouldn't bother you. You should rejoice that your mother is enjoying her freedom to do her own thing."

I then explained to him that if he had come to me with a protest based on biblical ethics, I could have supported his point of view, at least in part. Biblical law has something to say against insensitive parents provoking their children.

The young man had not thought through the implications of his ethic. He had no recourse when his thing came into conflict with someone else's thing. This is why laws are established to govern society. We seek laws that are inherently just, laws that are based on objective norms. Otherwise, we become victims of the unprincipled preferences of others.

One of the chief functions of law is to protect the rights of individuals. To be sure, every law restricts someone's freedom in order to protect someone else's rights. Laws against theft restrict the freedom of thieves while protecting the private-property rights of their intended victims. Laws against murder restrict the liberty of murderers to do their own thing.

The relevance of the United States Constitution and the Bill of Rights rests on the political theory that the nation is a republic and not a pure democracy. The difference between the two is crucial. It frequently has been summed up as the difference between rule by law and rule by men. In a pure democracy, the majority rules with complete authority. In a republic, the power and the freedom of the majority are restricted by law. The edicts of the Constitution are designed to protect the rights of every person from the power of the majority. For example, if the majority is of one race and decides to enact legislation that discriminates against a minority race, the minority can have the legislation overturned in court. In a republic, no one has the right to do his or her own thing if it violates the law.

For a republic to work, its foundational laws must be just. We can have tyranny by law as well as tyranny by men. That is why the founding fathers of the United States were acutely concerned about establishing just laws. But how do we know which laws are just and which laws are unjust—for example, in the case of abortion?

The issue of just and unjust laws is tied to ethics. Just laws reflect what is right. The very question of rights is rooted in the realm of ethics. We must be careful to distinguish between what we call moral rights and legal rights. In human societies, unjust laws may be passed. People may be given the legal right to do what is morally wrong or may be legally prohibited from doing what is either morally permissible or morally required. Thus, moral rights may be made illegal and immoral activities may become legal.

Who decides what is right?

To determine what is right about abortion, or about anything else, we must look beyond the laws of governments. Though legal opinions may be helpful and insightful, they do not constitute the highest court of appeals for determining what is ethically right.

The framers of the Declaration of Independence and the Constitution clearly appealed to norms beyond human legislation or judicial opinions in defining our most basic rights. Natural law was a chief consideration and served as a convenient middle ground to satisfy religious as well as nonreligious people. The religious person assumed that what God revealed in nature was compatible with and consistent with what He revealed in the Bible. The non-religious person was content to live by natural law as long as the canon law of the church was not made binding by the state.

Thus, the founders came to agreement on the common ground by which church and state could function together smoothly. That agreement, however, has radically disintegrated. Now, not only is biblical law under attack, but natural law has all but been eliminated as a foundation for societal law. The abortion issue is one manifestation of this ethical crisis.

To reach a national consensus on abortion will be a difficult if not impossible task. A large segment of the population will not look to the Bible for ethical norms, and many people believe that natural law is too vague to guide us on an ethical basis. A growing cynicism toward government indicates a reluctance to look there for ethical guidance. We are left with a kind of ethical free-for-all where deciding what is right is based on power alone, either by physical or electoral might.

Though the crisis of ethical relativism is real, its encroachment into society has not yet destroyed all hope of establishing justice on the objective norm of what is ethically right. We still have a Constitution in place. Though its credibility as an objective norm is being eroded by relativism, the Constitution still functions as an objective basis for law.

Whatever happens in the United States, however, will not change the nature of truth. Although the perception of reality may change from generation to generation, that does not change reality itself. Former generations perceived and believed that the earth was the center of the solar system; however, that did not have the slightest influence on either the sun or the earth. Neither did Copernicus alter the actual situation of the sun and the earth by the power of his theories.

Whatever happens to the Constitution or to American ethics will not determine when human life begins. That is an objective question, for better or for worse. But before we seek answers on the origin of life itself, an even broader issue—the sanctity of life—must be considered.

Summary

- The abortion issue is divisive and intertwined with other important cultural phenomena, including the women's movement and the sexual revolution.
- This is the core question of the abortion issue: Is abortion a form of murder?
- Many pro-abortion and pro-choice activists do not believe abortion is murder because they do not consider an unborn baby to be a living human person.
- Is a fetus a living person? When does life begin? These questions are foundational to any opinion about abortion.

- It is difficult for contemporary Americans to agree on what is right because the nation's laws increasingly have a relativistic base.

Discussion Questions

1. Why is abortion such a divisive issue?
2. How do people, whether anti-abortion, pro-choice, or pro-abortion, reach their positions? What kinds of criteria do they use?
3. What is attractive about "sitting on the fence" or taking a pro-choice position?
4. Would pure democracy be bad if we had a Christian majority? Why or why not?
5. What is the difference between a moral right and a legal right?
6. What role should the church take in relation to public policy?

Chapter Two

The Sanctity of Life

Once a man ceases to recognize the infinite value of the human soul . . . then all he can recognize is that man is something to be used. But then he will also have to go further and recognize that some men can no longer be utilized and he arrives at the concept that there are some lives that have no value at all.
—Helmut Thielicke

I do not feel that I am a product of chance, a speck of dust in the universe, but someone who was expected, prefigured. In short, a being whom only a creator could put here; and this idea of a creating hand refers to God.
—Jean-Paul Sartre

Any ethical matter that has life-and-death implications forces us to deal with the larger issue of the sanctity or sacredness of life. War, capital punishment, euthanasia, homicide, abortion, and health care—all are sanctity-of-life issues.

Since a central issue in the abortion debate is the question of when life begins, is the discussion clouded by introducing the matter of the overall sanctity of life? If, as already argued, pro-abortion and pro-choice activists do not consider abortion the destruction of human life, it may seem that all parties in the dispute have an equal concern for the sanctity of life. For the most part, the pro-abortion and pro-choice activists are not denying that life is sacred; they are only saying that a developing fetus is not a human life.

My intent in introducing the topic of the sanctity of life is not to muddle the issue of when life begins. The sanctity of life touches the abortion question when a person has real doubts about whether a fetus is a living human. Here's my reasoning: If we are in doubt at any point about whether or not we are dealing with human life in relation to abortion, the overarching principle of the sanctity of life stimulates us to think carefully and avoid rash judgments. The sanctity-of-life principle underscores the gravity of the question of when human life begins.

Though I am assuming that the majority of those who are pro-abortion or pro-choice declare a high view of the sanctity of life, it is wise to assume that the overall respect for the sanctity of life eroded significantly in the twentieth century.

Perhaps the most pressing issue in philosophy over the past century has been the question of anthropology, the nature of man. Pessimistic existential philosophy has raised serious questions about the value and worth of humanity. Jean-Paul Sartre once described man as a "useless passion." B. F. Skinner wondered aloud about the illusory character of human freedom. Friedrich

Nietzsche contemplated the dreadful depths of nihilism. Science has joined with philosophy and reached equally gloomy conclusions. Nuclear physicist Winston C. Duke stated: "A philosophy of reason will define a human being as life which demonstrates self-awareness, volition and rationality. Thus it should be recognized that not all men are human. . . . It would seem . . . to be more inhumane to kill an adult chimpanzee than a newborn baby, since the chimpanzee has greater mental awareness."[34]

Almost monthly we are alerted to new scientific discoveries that at once increase our understanding of the size and complexity of our universe and appear to diminish the role of man in the vast sum of things. More and more we appear to occupy a speck of an island in a vast cosmic sea.

People of ancient times were often awestruck by gazing toward the night sky. The vastness of what we see with our naked eye seems to dwarf our own locale by comparison. King David spoke of this thousands of years ago:

> O LORD, our Lord, how majestic is your name in all the
>   earth!
> You have set your glory above the heavens.
> Out of the mouth of babies and infants,
> you have established strength because of your foes,
> to still the enemy and the avenger.
> When I look at your heavens, the work of your fingers,
> the moon and the stars, which you have set in place,
> what is man that you are mindful of him,
> and the son of man that you care for him?

Yet you have made him a little lower than the heavenly
    beings
and crowned him with glory and honor. (Ps. 8:1–5)

If David was overwhelmed by the heavens, how much more
should we be with our modern understanding of the cosmos?
Philosopher Edward Carnell summed it up this way: "Modern
man appears to be but a grown-up germ, sitting on a gear of a
vast cosmic machine which is some day destined to cease functioning because of lack of power."[35]

This is not an optimistic view of the sanctity of human life.
Modern man contemplates the horror that he may live between
two poles: meaninglessness and insignificance. If our origin is
accidental and insignificant, and if our destiny is annihilation,
is it not absurd to believe that we have some significance in
between?

The nagging threat of insignificance propels some people to
religion, others to the occult, still others to forms of escapism,
and many to suicide. Yet most of us are not ready to give up on
the value of human life. All of our toil, struggles, longings for
significance, thoughts, and dreams force us to seek evidence for
our hope of human worth.

For years, I was active in labor-management relationships. I
saw over and over again that it is not economic issues that divide
these camps. The central issue is human dignity. Many times I
asked various groups: "How many of you want to be treated with
dignity? How many of you want to be valued as a person?" I
discovered that, though the makeup of such groups was diverse,

everyone wanted to be treated with dignity. Even if we have difficulty precisely defining the concept of dignity, we all understand what it means to lose it.

What, then, do we mean when we say that life is sacred? Does embracing the sanctity of anything mean that we must also embrace religion? The answer is both yes and no. To embrace anything as sacred requires that we first create a category for the sacred. Ultimately that requires some kind of religious framework. However, a secular society may use words with religious moorings that have been abandoned. Today when people speak of the sanctity of life, most mean simply that life has a special value or worth.

The Bible and the sanctity of life

In biblical terms, the sanctity of human life is rooted and grounded in creation. Mankind is not viewed as a cosmic accident but as the product of a carefully executed creation by an eternal God. Human dignity is derived from God. Man as a finite, dependent, contingent creature is assigned a high value by his Creator.

The creation account in Genesis provides the framework for human dignity: "Then God said, 'Let us make man in our image, after our likeness. And let them have dominion over the fish of the sea and over the birds of the heavens and over the livestock and over all the earth and over every creeping thing that creeps on the earth.' So God created man in his own image, in the image of God he created him; male and female he created them" (Gen. 1:26–27).

Creation in the image of God is what sets humans apart from all other creatures. The stamp of the image and likeness of God connects God and mankind uniquely. Though there is no biblical warrant for seeing man as godlike, there is a high dignity associated with this unique relationship to the Creator.

It has often been suggested that whatever dignity was given mankind through creation was erased or canceled through the fall. Since evil mars the countenance of human beings, is the original image still intact?

Because of the fall, something profound has stained the greatness of humanity. Therefore, we now must distinguish between the image of God in its wide and narrow senses.

The image of God in the narrow sense concerns mankind's ethical capacity and behavior. In creation, man was given the ability and the responsibility to mirror and reflect the holy character of God. Since the fall, the mirror has been splotched by the grime of sin. We have lost our capacity for moral perfection, but we have not lost our humanity with this ethical loss.

Man may no longer be pure, but he is still human. Insofar as we are still human, we retain the image of God in the wider sense. We are still valuable creatures. We may no longer be worthy, but we still have worth. This is the resounding biblical message of redemption. The creatures God created are the same creatures He is moved to redeem.

Because Christians speak so tirelessly about human sin, do they have a low view of humanity? Indeed, they have a low view of human virtue, but not a corresponding low view of human worth or importance. It is precisely because the Bible has such a high view of human dignity that Christians take human sin so seriously. If one rat steals another rat's food, we don't get morally outraged. But if one human steals another human's food, we rightly become concerned.

The biblical view indicates that human theft is more serious than rat theft because humans are a higher order of being. As the psalmist indicated, we are created "a little lower than the heavenly beings" (Ps. 8:5). This ranking of value is deeply rooted within our own humanity. For instance, when the president of the United States is killed, we do not refer to the deed merely as homicide or murder. We have a special word for it: *assassination.*

During the news reports that followed the announcement of the assassination of President Kennedy, the reporters seemed to have difficulty finding words powerful enough to express their outrage. They called the assassination "diabolical," "fiendish," "inhuman," and other such terms. I wondered at the time what made it difficult to describe Kennedy's murder simply as one human being killing another human being. Not only a devil or a fiend can commit murder. A person is not instantly shorn of humanity when he kills another human. Lee Harvey Oswald was a human being when he pulled the trigger in Dallas.

Does this mean, then, that in the hierarchy of value President Kennedy had more human dignity than Officer Tippet, who was killed the same day in the same city by the same man? By no means! The murder of Officer Tippet was just as much an assault on his dignity as the murder of Kennedy was on his. Each was a human person. Each had personal worth and dignity. Kennedy's person was no more laden with dignity than Tippet's.

What made the outrage over Kennedy's death greater than that over Tippet's death was the office Kennedy held. He was the president of the United States. He was the supreme *publica persona* of our land.

It is by similar reason that an offense against a human is more outrageous than an offense against a rat. Both the rat and the human are creatures created by God. But the "office" of a person is considerably higher than the "office" of the rat. It is mankind—not the rat—who is made in the image of God. It is the human who is given a role of dominion over the earth. Man, not the rat, is God's vice-regent over creation.

Does capital punishment violate the sanctity of life?

The principle of the special dignity of mankind is echoed later in Genesis in the institution of capital punishment: "Whoever sheds the blood of man, by man shall his blood be shed; for God made man in his own image" (Gen. 9:6).

This text is not a prophecy. It is not saying simply that those who live by the sword will die by the sword. Rather, the passage is a divine mandate for capital punishment in the case of murder. The significant point is that the moral basis for capital punishment in Genesis is the sanctity of life. The biblical ethic is that because man is endowed with the image of God, his life is so sacred that any malicious destruction of it must be punished by execution.

Note that this verse implies that an assault against human life is considered by God an assault against Himself. To murder a person is to attack one who is the image-bearer of God. God regards homicide as an implicit attempt to murder God.

The sanctity of life is reinforced and reaffirmed in the Ten Commandments. We read, "You shall not murder" (Ex. 20:13). The biblical prohibition against murder is widely known in our society. It is frequently appealed to as a moral ground against capital punishment. When the state of Pennsylvania voted to reinstate the death penalty for murder, the legislation was vetoed by then-Gov. Milton Shapp. Shapp explained to the news media that the ground for his veto was that the Ten Commandments said, "Thou shalt not kill."

Gov. Shapp should have read on. If we turn just a single page in Exodus, we see what the law of God required if someone broke the command prohibiting murder: "Whoever strikes a man so that he dies shall be put to death" (Ex. 21:12). The punitive measures against murder underscore the gravity of the crime precisely because of the value of the victim. Life is regarded as so sacred that it must never be destroyed without just cause.

Many Old Testament statements speak of the dignity of human life as it rests in divine creation, including the following:

"The Spirit of God has made me,
and the breath of the Almighty gives me life." (Job 33:4)

Know that the LORD, he is God!
It is he who made us, and we are his;
we are his people, and the sheep of his pasture. (Ps. 100:3)

"Woe to him who strives with him who formed him,
a pot among earthen pots!
Does the clay say to him who forms it, 'What are you
    making?'
Or 'Your work has no handles'?
Woe to him who says to a father, 'What are you
    begetting?'
or to a woman, 'With what are you in labor?'"
Thus says the LORD, the Holy One of Israel, and the
    one who formed him:
"Ask me of things to come;
will you command me concerning my children and the
    work of my hands?
I made the earth and created man on it;
It was my hands that stretched out the heavens,
and I commanded all their host." (Isa. 45:9–12)

But now, O LORD, you are our Father;
we are the clay, and you are our potter;
we are all the work of your hand. (Isa. 64:8)

Jesus' views on the sanctity of life

Interestingly, Jesus Christ gave the most important explanation
of the Old Testament view of the sanctity of life: "You have heard
that it was said to those of old, 'You shall not murder; and whoever
murders will be liable to judgment.' But I say to you that everyone
who is angry with his brother will be liable to judgment; whoever

insults his brother will be liable to the council; and whoever says, 'You fool!' will be liable to the hell of fire" (Matt. 5:21–22).

The words of Jesus have vital significance for our understanding of the sanctity of life. Here Jesus broadened the implications of the Old Testament law. He was speaking to religious leaders who had a narrow and simplistic grasp of the Ten Commandments. The legalists of His day were confident that if they obeyed the explicitly stated aspects of the law, they could applaud themselves for their great virtue. They failed, however, to grasp the wider implications. In Jesus' view, what the law did not spell out in detail was clearly implied by its broader meaning.

This quality of the law is seen in Jesus' expansion of the prohibition against adultery: "You have heard that it was said, 'You shall not commit adultery.' But I say to you that everyone who looks at a woman with lustful intent has already committed adultery with her in his heart" (Matt. 5:27–28). Here Jesus explained that a person who refrains from the physical act of adultery has not necessarily been obedient to the whole law. The law on adultery is a complex one, including not only actual illicit intercourse but everything that falls between lust and adultery. Jesus described lust as adultery of the heart.

The law not only prohibits certain negative behaviors and attitudes, but by implication it requires certain positive behaviors and attitudes. That is, if adultery is prohibited, chastity and purity are required.

When we apply these patterns set forth by Jesus to the prohibition against murder, we understand clearly that, on the one hand, we are to refrain from all things contained in the broad definition of murder, but on the other hand, we are positively commanded to work to save, improve, and care for life. We are to avoid murder in all of its ramifications and, at the same time, do all that we can to promote life.

Just as Jesus considered lust a part of adultery, so He viewed unjustifiable anger and slander as parts of murder. As lust is adultery of the heart, so anger and slander are murder of the heart.

By expanding the scope of the Ten Commandments to include such matters as lust and slander, Jesus did not mean that it is just as evil to lust after a person as it is to have unlawful physical intercourse. Likewise, Jesus did not say that slander is just as evil as murder. What He did say is that the law against murder includes a law against anything that involves injuring a fellow human unjustly.

How does all of this apply to the abortion issue? In Jesus' teaching we see another strong reinforcement of the sanctity of life. Murder of the heart, such as slander, may be described as "potential" murder. It is potential murder because, as an example, anger and slander have the potential to lead to the full act of physical murder. Of course, they do not always lead to that outcome. Anger and slander are prohibited, not so much because of what else they may lead to, but because of the actual harm they do to the quality of life.

The link between the sanctity of life and abortion

When we link the discussion of the sanctity of life to abortion, we make a subtle but relevant connection. Even if it cannot be proven that a fetus is an actual living human person, there is no doubt that it is a *potential* living human person. In other words, a fetus is a developing person. It is not in a frozen state of potentiality. The fetus is in dynamic process—without interference or unforeseen calamity, it surely will become a fully actualized living human person.

Jesus Christ sees the law against murder as including not only the act of actual murder, but also actions of potential murder. Jesus taught that it is unlawful to commit the potential murder of an actual life. What, then, are the implications of committing the actual destruction of potential life?

The actual destruction of potential life is not the same thing as the potential destruction of actual life. These are not identical cases, but they are close enough to make us pause to carefully consider the possible consequences before we destroy a potential life.

If this aspect of the law does not fully and finally capture abortion within the broad and complex prohibition against murder, a second aspect clearly does.

As I stated earlier, the negative prohibitions of the law imply positive attitudes and actions. For instance, the biblical law against adultery also requires chastity and purity. Likewise, when a law is stated in a positive form, its negative opposite is implicitly forbidden. For example, if God commands us to be good stewards of our money, clearly we ought not to be wild spenders. A positive command to diligent labor carries an implicit negative prohibition against being lazy on the job.

A negative prohibition against actual and potential murder implicitly involves a positive mandate to work for the protection and sustenance of life. To oppose murder is to promote life. Whatever else abortion does, it does not promote the life of the unborn child. Although some people will argue that abortion promotes the quality of life of those who do not desire offspring, it does not promote the life of the subject in question, the developing unborn child.

The Bible is consistently strong in its support for the exceedingly great value of all human life. The poor, the oppressed, the widowed, the orphaned, and the handicapped—all are highly valued in the Bible. Thus, any discussion of the abortion issue ultimately must wrestle with this key theme of Scripture. When the destruction or the disposal of even potential human life is done cheaply and easily, a shadow darkens the whole landscape of the sanctity of life and human dignity.

The sanctity of life, however, is not merely an issue of theological or religious law. It also touches heavily on matters of natural and positive law, which are subjects of the next chapter.

Summary

- The sanctity-of-life issue is important because it underscores the gravity of the debate over when life begins.
- Modern humanity is uncertain of its ultimate value and significance.
- The Bible has a high view of humanity's significance.

- The sanctity of life was articulated in the Old Testament, and its importance was expanded by Jesus Christ.
- Because the Bible is so emphatic in its support for the sanctity of life and human dignity, anyone contemplating abortion must ask, "Will my actions potentially align or conflict with biblical teaching?"

Discussion Questions

1. What influences have led to the weakening of Western society's sense of the sanctity of life?
2. Why do you want to be treated with dignity and respect?
3. If everyone agrees on the sanctity of life, why does the controversy over abortion remain?
4. What heroic attempt to protect, defend, or promote life has been in the news lately?
5. Does it make sense to execute murderers? Is such an act contradictory?

Chapter Three

The Sanctity of Life and Natural Law

I see no reason for attributing to man a significance in kind different from that which belongs to a baboon or a grain of sand.
—Oliver Wendell Holmes

The opinion (Roe v. Wade) *fails even to consider what I would suppose to be the most compelling interest of the state in prohibiting abortion: the interest in maintaining that respect for the paramount sanctity of human life which has always been at the center of Western civilization.*
—Archibald Cox

A high regard for human life is not the exclusive legacy of Christianity or other religious faiths. In the natural law arising in many cultures, in belief systems, and in nature itself, we find a persistent devotion to the sanctity of life.

Natural law is rooted in various sources. One source is the laws of nations. When the laws, taboos, and precepts found in diverse cultures in various ages are examined, regular patterns of law become apparent. For example, in virtually every culture of recorded history, some evidence is found of laws against murder. There are some societies, or groups within societies, that condone or enjoin murder (such as within Satanic worship cults or militant terrorist cabals), but even within such groups, the condoned murder tends to be highly selective. Murder may be approved for one's enemies but not for the members of the group themselves. Here we find a kind of "honor among thieves."

A second source of natural law is what philosophers call "first principles," or clear and distinct ideas. The national documents of the United States call these ideas "self-evident" truths. The impropriety of the act of murder is seen as one of these self-evident truths. Murder violates what Immanuel Kant defined as the "Categorical Imperative," which involves a kind of universal sense of duty or "oughtness." Kant's formulation sounds very much like the Golden Rule expressed in more philosophical language. The Golden Rule, simply stated, is "Do unto others as you would have others do unto you." If we apply this rule to the sanctity of life, it means, "I should refrain from committing murder if I want others to refrain from murdering me."

A third and vitally important source for natural law is the universal biological law of self-preservation. In the complexities of nature, living organisms make a herculean effort to stay alive and to reproduce. Two of the premises basic to Darwinian evolution are the quests for survival and for reproduction, to which the concept of natural selection is linked.

Timothy Ferris, in *Coming of Age in the Milky Way*, cited the example of moths living in a forest in England. Of the varieties of moths, the overwhelming majority were white. A very small number of black moths were counted. Then something radically altered the moths' environment. A factory was built on the edge of a town near the forest. Black smoke belched daily from the chimneys of the factory, leaving a residue of soot on the bark of the trees. Within a few years, the moth population changed dramatically. The black moths became the dominant variety, while the white moths all but disappeared. The darkened tree trunks afforded excellent coverage for the black moths, allowing them to live long enough to reproduce, while the white moths were clearly visible to their natural enemies and began to die off before they could reproduce. Those moths that won the battle for survival became the dominant variety.

Consider the case of the common dandelion. One dandelion in a lawn is not much to be concerned about. But as every homeowner knows, where there is one dandelion, soon there will be many more. As the dandelion goes to seed, it forms the fuzzy head that children like to blow. The slightest wind scatters the tiny seeds. Some fall on the sidewalk and perish, but many land on fertile soil, germinate, and produce a sea of yellow.

Why doesn't the dandelion produce only one or two seeds? Dandelions do not buy the Planned Parenthood theory that the perfect family involves a maximum of two children. The multitude of seeds that the dandelion sends into the air is nature's way of ensuring the survival of the species. The dandelion lottery is weighted for success.

In the case of human reproduction, the force of nature is even more astonishing. A fertile female produces one egg per month. In itself, this does not seem like a prolific number designed to enhance the species' survival. Yet during human intercourse, in a single male ejaculation (depending on the man's age and fertility), between thirty million and sixty million sperm are released toward the target egg. If one sperm seed penetrates the egg, fertilization takes place. It almost seems like overkill. Nature, in terms of human reproduction, leaves little to chance. The female egg is subjected to a bombardment of male sperm to increase the likelihood of fertilization.

Once the egg is fertilized, crisis stages must be passed successfully before a child can be born. First, the fertilized egg must be successfully implanted in the womb. A significant percentage of fertilized eggs fail to achieve implantation. Of those that implant, another percentage fail to develop to term as they are lost through natural abortion or miscarriage. Of the fetuses that make it through the entire gestation process, some fail to survive the birth process and are stillborn. Of the babies that are born alive, some die in early infancy.

We see that the production of a healthy living baby is one of nature's most amazing feats. How high are the odds against a single sperm ever contributing to the life of a human being? Yet it happens.

We can look at the probability quotient of human reproduction in different ways. Suppose, for example, a couple had a great desire to have a child and decided to make a concerted effort to effect a pregnancy. Suppose they had intercourse every day for thirty days. In that thirty-day period, the odds against a particular sperm yielding a fertilized egg would be on average over a billion to one. Add the factors of failed implantation, miscarriage, and so on, and the approximate odds against a particular sperm's being a contributory factor to a live baby would be about two billion to one—if pregnancy were achieved in the thirty-day attempt. Many couples try earnestly for not just one month but for years before achieving pregnancy.

Looking at the odds in this way makes it seem that human reproduction is an almost impossible task. That is because we are looking at it from the perspective of a single sperm. But nature provides millions, indeed billions, of sperm, or "genetic bullets," in order to make sure the target egg is hit. Nature operates a system of human reproduction that ensures the survival of the species.

Abortion versus nature

Abortion—whatever else it may be—is an act against nature. After all the elaborate processes have worked together to produce a fertilized and implanted egg, then a developing human embryo, the natural process is interrupted and frustrated by the willful act of a human being. In this instance, humanity's greatest enemy in the cycle of nature's law of self-preservation and survival is humanity itself.

The natural law of self-preservation is seen not only in human reproduction but also in the struggle among humans to survive illnesses, accidents, and other perils. A vivid example of this effort was seen in the energy exerted to save the life of a little girl named Jessica who fell into a well in Texas. For days, Americans monitored the television bulletins for news of the child's fate. No expense was spared, no effort deemed too great to save Jessica's life. Her rescue was not just extraordinary altruism, but a sign of the deep-rooted commitment within humanity to spare no effort to save a human life, especially when the life is that of a child.

Whenever a crisis occurs, our first concern is for the people involved. What happened? Is everyone all right? Was anyone hurt? Did help arrive in time? Is there anything we can do? It doesn't really matter whether it was a natural disaster or a terrorist attack. It isn't particularly important whether it was an accident or a crime. It makes no real difference whether it was a national calamity or a personal tragedy. Our first thought is always of the people.

People are precious. Their lives are of inestimable value. They are gifts. They must never be taken for granted. Things can be replaced—but there is no replacement for a mother, a father, a sister, a brother, an aunt, an uncle, a friend, or a neighbor. Civil societies always recognize this vital principle and build their cultural institutions upon it. They do anything and everything they possibly can to protect the dignity, integrity, and sanctity of life. Because there are no expendable or disposable people, every life is worth honoring, protecting, and saving. Ultimately, the rule of law depends on an absolute respect for the value of people.

Why do we display this kind of concern for living individuals but not for the multitude of unborn who die each day and become mere statistics? Perhaps the reason is that people outside the womb are not nameless, abstract statistics. In little Jessica's case, we saw pictures of her face. We knew her name. We heard interviews with her distraught mother and father. By television, we became personally acquainted. Jessica was a real person. However, in the case of abortion, we are not so personally acquainted. Many people do not consider fetuses to be people at all, or at least they are not sure whether fetuses are people. The unborn remain anonymous "things" that are discarded. Fetuses have no names. They have no personal biographies. They tend to be presented to the public mind as abstract entities. I have heard fetuses described in abortion debates as "undifferentiated blobs of protoplasm," "biological parasites," and "so much domestic sewage."

It is difficult for people to become concerned about the fate of blobs of protoplasm or domestic sewage. After a child is born, no one is much concerned about the destiny of the placenta. Perhaps this demonstrates why the film *The Silent Scream* provoked such an outcry. In this film, viewers had a window into the womb that revealed a graphic picture of what actually happens in an abortion. Pro-abortion activists decried the film as emotionally provocative and inflammatory. They were certainly correct in that assessment. The film was indeed emotionally provocative, precisely because what was once hidden from the human eye was made clearly visible.

In *The Silent Scream*, we saw what looked like a formed human being going though obvious pain and distress in trying to escape the destructive instruments of the abortionist. The face was contorted into what resembled agonized human pain. The mouth opened in what looked like a human scream. Those factors were indeed emotionally provocative. The drama on screen did not resemble removal of a "tumor" or a "parasite" from a human body.

The fact that people become emotional about the abortion issue has a rational basis. The emotion is not arbitrary or capricious. The emotion is rooted in the deep human consciousness of the sanctity of life. It is emotional concern for the well-being of people—living people. Granted, many people remain unconvinced that the fetus is a human person. But if a fetus is a living person, or even if it is merely perceived to be, the emotional response should not be considered irrational.

The sanctity of life in American history

The foundational documents of the United States' system of government give eloquent testimony to the sanctity of human life. The Declaration of Independence affirms that it is "self-evident" that we are endowed by our Creator with "certain inalienable rights," among which are "life, liberty, and the pursuit of happiness." The right of each person to life is seen as basic to all other human rights. Obviously, if the right to life were not primary, no other human rights would mean very much.

What was affirmed by the Declaration of Independence was encoded in the United States Constitution. The Fifth Amendment of the Constitution reads:

No person shall be held to answer for a capital or otherwise infamous crime, unless on a presentment or indictment of a Grand Jury, except in cases arising in the land or naval forces, or in the Militia, when in actual service in time of War or public danger; nor shall any person be subject for the same offence to be twice put in jeopardy of life or limb, nor shall be compelled in any criminal case to be a witness against himself, nor be deprived of life, liberty, or property, without due process of law; nor shall private property be taken for public use without just compensation.

The chief intent of this amendment is due process of law, but it evidences a concern for life, liberty, and private property. It is because of the constitutional commitment to the sanctity of life that personal liberty and property are thus protected.

It is important to note that because of the *Roe v. Wade* decision of the Supreme Court, developing fetuses are not accorded protection under this constitutional amendment—nor any other amendment—because they are not deemed to be people till they reach the point of viability (able to survive outside the womb). At the present time, though the law of the United States affirms the principle of the sanctity of human life, that principle does not include or embrace the unborn, because the unborn are not considered alive.

The history of abortion

The law codes of various nations throughout history have included strong affirmations of the sanctity of human life. However, there is a disparity on the question of abortion. Though some nations have included the unborn under the sanctions that protect human life, many nations have not. In the sense that the United States' position has changed at least twice on this point[36]—and may yet change again—this country is a microcosm of the disparity on this issue that has existed throughout world history.

The ancient world was divided over abortion. The Greeks debated the issue strenuously and are considered pioneers in legalized abortion. Michael J. Gorman notes, "The Greeks enjoy the dubious distinction of being the first [in the ancient Near East or Western world] positively to advise and even demand abortion in certain cases."[37] Plato recommended both abortion and infanticide when it was necessary to advance the interests of the state. However, though Greek philosophers tended to support abortion, the medical community tended to oppose it. Abortion is specifically mentioned in the famous Oath of Hippocrates, which reads as follows:

I swear by Apollo Physician, by Asclepias, by Health, by Panacea, and by all the gods and goddesses, making them my witnesses, that I will carry out, according to my ability and judgment, this oath and this indenture. . . . I will use treatment to help the sick according to my ability and judgment, but never with a view to injury and wrongdoing. Neither will I administer a poison to anybody when asked to do so, nor will I suggest such a course. Similarly, I will not give to a woman a pessary to cause abortion.[38]

Roman law, for the most part, did not outlaw abortion, as the fetus was not considered a living person. Some philosophers, such as Cicero, objected to this, but Roman law was not changed.

The Jews did not sanction abortion; likewise, the early Christian community was unambiguous on the question. The earliest explicit inferences to abortion in Christian literature are found in the *Didache* and *The Epistle of Barnabas*. The *Didache* was a manual of church discipline and a codebook for Christian morality. It was called a summary of the teaching of the apostles. It probably was written at the beginning of the second century. The *Didache* contrasts two ways or styles of living. One is called the way of life and the other is called the way of death. In the second commandment of the teaching, we read this exhortation: "Do not murder; do not commit adultery; do not corrupt boys; do not fornicate; do not steal; do not practice magic; do not go in for sorcery; do not murder a child by abortion or kill a new-born infant."[39]

Likewise, *The Epistle of Barnabas* declares, "Thou shalt not murder a child by abortion."[40]

It is noteworthy that in the ancient cultures where abortion was legal, infanticide was legal as well. The Jewish and Christian communities outlawed both.[41] Indeed, history reveals that where Jewish and Christian influence was felt on national policies, the tendency was to include the unborn under the general concept of the sanctity of life.

Again, it is clear that the overarching issue is the question of when human life begins. Though the sanctity of life in general may be seen as an integral part of the laws of nations, the question of the beginning of life is not settled by law.

Summary

- The sanctity of life is affirmed by the laws of nations, self-evident truths, and natural science.
- The human reproductive system exhibits a tremendous bias toward life.
- It is rational to view abortion as an emotional issue.
- The *Roe v. Wade* Supreme Court decision voided protection of the nonviable unborn under the Fifth Amendment of the United States Constitution.
- In the ancient world, Greeks and Romans supported abortion and infanticide, but the Jewish and Christian communities did not.

Discussion Questions

1. If the Bible clearly demonstrates a high regard for the sanctity of life, do we need to be concerned about what natural law says?
2. Which argument for the sanctity of life is most compelling to a Christian? Which would be most compelling to an unbeliever?
3. Where have you seen the principle of the sanctity of human life upheld in legal decisions and law enforcement?
4. Why do pro-abortion activists speak of "undifferentiated blobs of protoplasm" or "biological parasites"? Why were they outraged by the movie *The Silent Scream?*

Chapter Four

When Does Life Begin?

*Each of us had been a Tom Thumb in the womb of the mother,
and women have always known that there was a kind
of underground country, a kind of vaulted shelter, with
a kind of red light and curious noise in which very tiny humans
were having a very curious and marvelous life.
That is the story of Tom Thumb.*
—Jerome Lejeune, M.D., Ph.D.

The question of when life begins is tightly linked to the secret of life itself.

I have a cousin who is a physician and who served as chief of staff at a metropolitan hospital. I once quizzed him about the search for a cure for cancer. "With all the advanced technology at our disposal and with the use of computers in research, why aren't we advancing more rapidly in our quest for a cure for cancer?" I asked. My cousin explained that to discover the secret of cancer requires that we discover the secret of life, because cancer is a form of life. It is life run amuck, but it is life.

As difficult as it may be to unravel the secret of life, it may be equally difficult to define it. Concepts such as *human, living,* and *person* have been the subject of much discussion and analysis. Plato sought desperately for a description that would clearly distinguish humans from all other species of animals. He finally chose "featherless biped" as his working definition. This lasted only until one of Plato's students threw a plucked chicken over the academy wall with an attached note that read, "Plato's man."

When we turn to the Bible, we discover that it offers no explicit statement that life begins at a certain point or that there is human life before birth. However, Scripture assumes a continuity of life from before the time of birth to after the time of birth. The same language and the same personal pronouns are used indiscriminately for both stages. Further, God's involvement in the life of the person extends back to conception (and even before conception). This passage supports the point:

> For you formed my inward parts;
> you knitted me together in my mother's womb.
> I praise you, for I am fearfully and wonderfully made.
> Wonderful are your works;
> my soul knows it very well.
> My frame was not hidden from you,
> when I was being made in secret,
> intricately woven in the depths of the earth.
> Your eyes saw my unformed substance;

in your book were written, every one of them,
the days that were formed for me,
when as yet there was none of them. (Ps. 139:13–16)

The psalmist credits God for fashioning him in the womb. He also uses the term *me* to refer to himself before he was born. It is noteworthy that the Hebrew word translated as "unformed substance" is the Hebrew word for "embryo," and this is the only instance of that word in the Bible.

Another passage relevant to God's involvement in life within the womb occurs in Isaiah:

Listen to me, O coastlands,
and give attention, you peoples from afar.
The Lord called me from the womb,
from the body of my mother he named my name.
He made my mouth like a sharp sword;
in the shadow of his hand he hid me;
he made me a polished arrow;
in his quiver he hid me away.
And he said to me, "You are my servant,
Israel, in whom I will be glorified."
But I said, "I have labored in vain;
I have spent my strength for nothing and vanity;
yet surely my right is with the Lord,
and my recompense with my God."
And now the Lord says, he who formed me from the
    womb to be his servant,

> to bring Jacob back to him; and that Israel might be
>   gathered to him—
> for I am honored in the eyes of the LORD, and my God
>   has become my strength. (Isa. 49:1–5)

This passage indicates not only that the unborn baby was distinct from the mother and was treated with a unique personal identity, but that his formation in the womb was the activity of God.

A similar treatment concerns the prophet Jeremiah:

> Now the word of the LORD came to me, saying,
> "Before I formed you in the womb I knew you,
> and before you were born I consecrated you;
> I appointed you as a prophet to the nations." (Jer. 1:4–5)

Jeremiah is told that God knew him before he was born; God had personal knowledge of the person of Jeremiah before the person Jeremiah was born. This indicates that Jeremiah was treated by God in a personal manner and as a personal being before birth. It is also significant that God "set apart" or sanctified Jeremiah before birth. Clearly God extends the sanctity principle to life in the womb.

Even those who do not agree that life begins before birth grant that there is continuity between a child that is conceived and a child that is born. Every child has a past before birth. The issue is this: Was that past personal or impersonal, with personhood beginning only at birth? It is clear that Scripture regards personhood as beginning prior to birth. As David says, "Behold, I was brought forth in iniquity, and in sin did my mother conceive me" (Ps. 51:5).

Professor John Frame, in *Medical Ethics*, made the following observation on Psalm 51:5:

> Personal continuity extends back in time to the point of conception. Psalm 51:5 clearly and strikingly presses this continuity back to the point of conception. In this passage David is reflecting on the sin in his heart that had recently taken the form of adultery and murder. He recognizes that the sin of his heart is not itself a recent phenomenon but goes back to the point of his conception in the womb of his mother. . . . The personal continuity between David's fetal life and his adult life goes back as far as conception and extends even to this ethical relation to God.[42]

In Psalm 51, David recounts his personal moral history to the point of conception. An impersonal being, a "blob of protoplasm," cannot be a moral agent. If David's moral history extends back to conception, then his personal history also must extend to the same point. It is not merely David's biological substance that dates back to conception, but his moral disposition as well.

The New Testament provides a fascinating text that has bearing on the question of life before birth:

> [Mary] entered the house of Zechariah and greeted Elizabeth. When Elizabeth heard the greeting of Mary,

the baby leaped in her womb. And Elizabeth was filled
with the Holy Spirit, and she exclaimed with a loud cry,
"Blessed are you among women, and blessed is the fruit
of your womb! And why is this granted to me that the
mother of my Lord should come to me? For behold,
when the sound of your greeting came to my ears, the
baby in my womb leaped for joy." (Luke 1:40–44)

This passage describes the meeting between Mary, the
mother of Jesus Christ, and her cousin Elizabeth, who was pregnant with John the Baptist. Upon their meeting, John, while
still in the womb of his mother, leaped for joy. This behavior
was consistent with the designated prophetic role of John, who
was commissioned by God to "announce" the Messiah. In this
instance, John performed his prophetic duty before either he or
Jesus was born. These verses show that before John was born,
he exhibited cognition and emotion. He leaped because he was
in a state of joy. The joy was prompted by his recognition of the
presence of the Messiah.

Some people may dismiss the relevance of this passage on the
grounds that (1) the writer is speaking poetically or hyperboli-
cally; (2) the passage says nothing about life from conception,
only about life prior to birth; or (3) the occasion represents a
special miracle and does not prove that other babies could have
such prenatal ability.

To answer the first objection, it is erroneous to dismiss the
passage on the grounds that it is poetic or hyperbolic. The lit-
erary form of this portion of Luke's Gospel is unambiguously

historical narrative, not poetry. Also, hyperbole is an exaggerated statement of reality. If this incident is presented with hyperbole, that simply means John did not leap as high or recognize as much as the text implies.

The second objection, that the passage says nothing of conception as the beginning point of life, is correct. The passage clearly indicates, however, that John had human powers of cognition and emotion (signs of personality) prior to birth.

The third objection, that this incident was a special miracle, is more weighty. Unless we claim that a normal fetus has the ability to recognize the near presence of another fetus in another woman's womb, we must concede that there is something extraordinary or miraculous about this occurrence. It is possible that God miraculously enabled the prenatal John to have extraordinary cognitive powers that do not belong to average unborn children. However, if we grant the miracle, we are still left with a difficult question: Was the miracle an act of *extending* normal powers beyond the normal limits or an act of *creating* the powers? Did the unborn John the Baptist have the natural abilities of cognition and emotion, abilities that were extended by a miracle, or were the very powers of cognition and emotion created by God? There is no way to answer that question absolutely.

However, before we dismiss the passage in Luke, two observations must be made. In many other biblical miracles, we see God extending powers or abilities that already exist. For example, in 2 Kings 6:15–17, God opened the eyes of the servant of Elisha so that he could see an angelic host. God did not first miraculously have to give the servant the power to see. Rather, the limit of his natural ability to see was extended. Likewise, for John to recognize Jesus Christ while each was still in his mother's womb, God did not necessarily have to create the powers of cognition and emotion.

The second observation is that, however we evaluate this incident, one thing is certain: John the Baptist was an unborn child who manifested cognition and joy.

Now let's consider the most controversial biblical reference to the abortion issue, which is found in Exodus 21:22–25:

> "When men strive together and hit a pregnant woman, so
> that her children come out, but there is no harm, the one
> who hit her shall surely be fined, as the woman's husband
> shall impose on him, and he shall pay as the judges deter-
> mine. But if there is harm, then you shall pay life for life,
> eye for eye, tooth for tooth, hand for hand, foot for foot,
> burn for burn, wound for wound, stripe for stripe."

In this text, there is a difficult ambiguity related to the phrase "no harm." No harm to whom? Some people believe this text means that if, in the midst of a struggle by two men, a woman was hurt and miscarried, a fine could be levied to compensate for the loss of the child, and if the woman was seriously injured or killed, the penalty should correspond to her injury. Others interpret this text to teach that the unborn baby was less valuable under the law than the woman, and was therefore less than human.

If this second interpretation of the text is correct, we must note that the fetus nevertheless was protected by law. Its destruction did merit some punishment—though not capital punishment—and it was accorded value. Also, if the accidental miscarriage was seen as a serious matter, it would seem that *intentional* destruction of the fetus would be even more serious. In the case envisioned in Exodus, it was obviously not the intention of the mother that her baby should be aborted. She was to be compensated for the loss of a child that she did not desire to lose. (Nothing is said about compensation or punishment in the case of intentional abortion.)

A third major interpretation of the text holds that it is not talking about the death or loss of a fetus but of a forced premature birth. The idea is this: If two men fought, and in the scuffle they injured a woman who was pregnant to the extent that she went into labor and bore a child prematurely, with no serious injury to the child, then the mother and father were to receive compensatory payment for their inconvenience. But if the prematurely born child suffered further harm, then the full law applied: "life for life, eye for eye, tooth for tooth," and so on. This means that if the baby died, a capital crime had occurred.

A more comprehensive treatment of this text is found in *Medical Ethics*. Frame points out that this last, broader interpretation of the text does not help the pro-abortion argument. He provides careful exegesis of the Hebrew terms to demonstrate that a narrower understanding is more accurate.[43]

The Bible clearly indicates that unborn babies are considered living human beings before they are born. The weight of the biblical evidence is that life begins at conception.

How human life develops

The development of a human being is a process that begins at conception and continues until death. No one would argue that human development begins at birth.

The moment of conception combines forty-six genes—twenty-three from the mother and twenty-three from the father—so that a unique individual begins the process of personal human development. After two weeks, there is a discernible heartbeat. The heart circulates blood within the embryo that is not the mother's blood, but blood the unborn baby has produced.

After about six weeks, the embryo is still less than an inch long but has undergone considerable development. Fingers have formed on the hands. At forty-three days, the unborn baby has detectable brain waves. After six and a half weeks, the embryo is moving; however, because of the tiny size of the unborn baby and the thickness of the mother's abdominal wall, she does not sense "quickening" or movement until several weeks later.

By the end of nine weeks, the fetus has developed a unique set of fingerprints. By this time, the sexual organs of the male have already appeared so that the gender of the unborn baby can be distinguished. The kidneys also have formed and are functioning.[44]

By the end of the tenth week, the gallbladder is functioning. All the organs of the body are functional by the end of the twelfth week, and the baby can cry. All of this is accomplished during the first three months of pregnancy.

In adults, heartbeat and brain waves are commonly referred to as "vital" signs. When both brain waves and the heartbeat cease for a period of time, a patient may be declared legally dead. Vital signs are a demonstration of life. When such signs are clearly present in the developing embryo, why are people so reluctant to speak of prenatal life? The embryo or fetus is not yet an independent living human person, but that does not mean he or she is not a living human person. If independence is the critical criterion for distinguishing living people from living nonpeople, then we must admit (as some readily do) that even birth does not yield a living person. At birth, the baby is disconnected physically from the mother—and in that sense is independent—but a newborn is still desperately dependent on outside help for survival. The newborn can breathe by himself in most cases, but he cannot feed himself.

What death reveals about life

In our quest to understand the presence of life, it is helpful to have an understanding of death. Since death is the cessation of life, it gives clues into the essential elements of life itself.

One problem with our definitions of life and death is seen in the case of stillborn babies. Are stillborn babies "dead babies" or "never-have-been-alive babies"? It is commonplace for physicians to speak of stillborn babies as babies who have died.

My daughter delivered a stillborn baby. I will relate her experience to show how a nonreligious community dealt with the event. In the ninth month of her pregnancy, my daughter noticed that an entire day had passed with no feeling of fetal movement. She called her doctor, who examined her immediately. His response was grim: "I am sorry, but your baby has died," he told my daughter. The physician used the language of death to describe the event.

The next day, my daughter was admitted to the hospital and labor was induced. She endured the labor experience knowing in advance that she would give birth to a stillborn baby. After the baby—a girl—was delivered, the nurses cleansed the body and took photographs. The baby was given a name, and measurements were recorded in the hospital records. The nurses then brought the dead child into my daughter's room—giving her, her husband, my wife, and me the opportunity to hold the baby. This was not an extraordinary or macabre experience, but the customary practice. The nurses explained that giving the parents an opportunity to hold the stillborn baby and to say "goodbye" made the grief process for the lost child less severe.

Holding my daughter's stillborn baby was a profound experience for me. Though I already was convinced that unborn babies are living human beings, any shadow of doubt I might have had was instantly removed. As I held the child, I wondered how anyone could think that the baby was not a human being then or two days earlier.

We use this expression: "If it looks like a duck and it walks like a duck, it probably is a duck." In the case of human fetuses, we are definitely not talking about ducks. The fetus looks like a living human person. It acts like a human person. The embryo has the genetic structure of a human person. It has the vital signs of a living human person. The fetus has sexuality and movement.

Often, it sucks its thumb, reacts to music, and kicks its legs. With this cumulative evidence, it would seemingly require powerful evidence to the contrary to conclude that a prenatal baby is not a living human person. Why do people resist this conclusion?

The answer is prejudice. Indeed, prejudice is a powerful force in the debate concerning abortion. If we regard the embryo or fetus as a living human person, then the moral implications of destroying that person prior to birth are enormous. As long as we can convince ourselves that a fetus is not human until birth, we are relieved of those difficulties.

Even if we come to the conclusion that an embryo is a living human person prior to birth, we have still not established that life begins at conception. All we have established is that life begins before birth. The most clear lines of demarcation in the continuum between conception and birth are the conception and birth themselves. If we grant that a fetus is a living human person merely five minutes, or even five seconds, before birth, then birth cannot be the point when life begins.

In my judgment, the evidence from science is as weighty as that inferred from the Bible that a fetus is a living human person prior to birth. If that is so, then we must locate the beginning of that life either at the point of conception or at some point between conception and birth.

The view of law on when life begins

In its *Roe v. Wade* decision in 1973, the Supreme Court ruled that the state cannot regulate abortion in the first trimester of pregnancy and left the decision to the woman and her physician. In the second trimester, the state may choose to regulate abortion, but only to protect the woman's health. In the third trimester, the state may choose to regulate or prohibit abortion except if it is necessary to preserve the woman's health or life. In summary, the court held that although the state has an important and legitimate interest in protecting potential life, this interest cannot become compelling until the point at which the fetus is viable.

In the *Roe v. Wade* decision, it appears that the court regarded the unborn as having only "potential" life until the point of viability. Supreme Court Justice Sandra Day O'Connor raised questions about this:

> The difficulty with this analysis is clear: Potential life is no less potential in the first weeks of pregnancy than it is at viability or afterwards.... The choice of viability as the point at which the state interest in potential life becomes compelling is no less arbitrary than choosing any point before viability or any point afterward. Accordingly, I believe that the state's interest in protecting potential human life exists throughout the pregnancy.[45]

Justice O'Connor sharply located the problem with the court's decision. In addressing a matter of life and death, the court ruled in an arbitrary manner. The so-called point of viability is a highly unstable point of reference. In the years since *Roe v. Wade*, the point of viability has been moved several weeks earlier and continues to change as medical technology raises the survival rate of prematurely born infants.

Even more problematic, the *Roe v. Wade* decision rested largely on a perceived constitutional right to privacy guaranteed in the Ninth and Fourteenth amendments. Robert Bork explains that this "right" was created by mere judicial fiat. Justice Harry Blackmun, in writing the majority opinion for *Roe v. Wade*, nearly conceded this point: "This right to privacy, whether it be founded in the Fourteenth Amendment's concept of personal liberty and restrictions upon state action, as we feel it is, or, as District Court determined, in the Ninth Amendment's reservation of rights to the people, is broad enough to encompass a woman's decision whether or not to terminate her pregnancy."[46]

Bork concluded: "That is it. This is the crux of the opinion. The Court did not even feel obliged to settle the question of where the right of privacy or the subsidiary right to abort is to be attached to the Constitution's text. The opinion seems to regard that as a technicality that really does not matter, and indeed it does not since the right does not come out of the Constitution but is forced into it."[47]

The abortion debate on the legal and judicial front seems destined to continue. The dissenting opinion to *Roe v. Wade*, written by Justice Byron White, reflects the continuing concern:

> I find nothing in the language or history of the Constitution to support the Court's judgment. The Court simply fashions and announces a new constitutional right for pregnant mothers and, with scarcely any reason

or authority for its action, invests that with sufficient substance to override most existing state abortion statutes. The upshot is that the people and the legislatures of the 50 states are constitutionally disentitled to weigh the relative importance of the continued existence and development of the fetus, on the one hand, against the spectrum of possible impacts on the mother, on the other hand. As an exercise of raw judicial power, the Court perhaps has authority to do what it does today; but in my view its judgment is an improvident and extravagant exercise of the power of judicial review that the Constitution extends to this Court.[48]

As the debate on the legality of abortion continues, the central issue will be the question of when human life begins. So much is at stake that we must ask, "What should we do if we remain unsure of the answer?"

Summary

- The question of when life begins is made more difficult to answer because it is linked tightly to the meaning of life itself.
- Scripture does not offer an explicit statement as to when life begins. Implicitly, Scripture supports the idea that life begins at conception.

- Science offers compelling evidence for the early personal human development of the child in the womb.
- The Supreme Court's *Roe v. Wade* decision arbitrarily fixed "viability" as the point where the state has important and compelling reasons to protect human life.

Discussion Questions

1. Why is the issue of when life begins so critical?
2. What impact does understanding early fetal development have on our position?
3. How clear is the Bible on when life begins? How clear is science?
4. Will the battle over abortion be finished if everyone becomes convinced that life begins at conception?

Chapter Five

What If You Are Not Sure About Abortion?

*People who worry about the moral danger of abortion do so because
they think of the fetus as a human being and hence equate feticide
with murder. Whether the fetus is or is not a human being is a
matter of definition, not fact, and we can define any way we wish.*
—Garrett Hardin

*Never will I sit motionless while directly or indirectly apology is
made for the murder of the helpless. In securing any kind of peace,
the first essential is to guarantee to every man the most elementary
of rights: the right to his own life. Murder is not debatable.*
—Theodore Roosevelt

Though the two camps, the pro-abortion and pro-life positions,
are adamant and have a high level of certainty in their views,
multitudes of people are still seeking their own conclusions
in the abortion matter. Even among those who have reached

a conclusion, it is frequently tentative at best. There remains an openness to be persuaded of a different view. The fact that opinions on this issue do change can be seen in the astonishing movement in public opinion regarding abortion since 1973.

I think it is safe to assume that prior to *Roe v. Wade* public opinion ran overwhelmingly against abortion. Through the 1970s and '80s, societal attitudes shifted to a much more tolerant position. From 1990 to the present, the trend has shifted back slightly, so that a slim majority of Americans now oppose unrestricted abortion on demand. Why is this?

Surely the issue has been discussed more frequently and more deeply than at any time in history. This factor might bode pessimism for the pro-life position. If increased discussion has not served to stem the tide of public opinion substantially, could it be that the case against abortion is weak and that the more we argue the pro-life position, the more ground we lose? I doubt it. Another factor may be a backlash against violence perpetrated by zealous pro-life activists. Yet another reason may be that as the discussions continue and the complexities of the issue become more apparent, more and more people seek the "safe" pro-choice position because they lack sufficient certainty to decide for either the pro-abortion or pro-life position.

Although all of these may be contributing factors, I submit that the greatest cause of the change of public opinion is the Supreme Court's decision in *Roe v. Wade*. There is a strong tendency among people of any nation to take their direction as to what is ethically right from what the law allows or what the society condones. The unspoken assumption is that if it is legal, it is therefore moral. Sadly, this conclusion does not reflect much sober thinking or ethical analysis, yet the syndrome is repeated in culture after culture. We still wonder how the people of Germany could have been duped into supporting the programs of Adolf Hitler, but it is a fact of history that they were. Once a decision has been reached in a nation's highest court, that decision's subsequent influence on the shaping of public opinion is enormous. We learned this painful fact in the years that followed the Supreme Court's infamous *Dred Scott v. Sandford* decision (1857), which perpetuated slavery in the United States.

The United States has reversed itself on slavery, prohibition, racial discrimination, conscientious objection to wars, capital punishment, and other issues of ethics and justice. Some people regard these shifts in public policy as reflective of the dynamic character of social mores and ethics. Those who are skeptical about the possibility of discovering absolutes in the areas of justice and ethics view these shifts as part of the process of sociological evolution. Thus, contemporary community standards become the highest court of appeal, the ultimate norm of justice and ethics.

Assuming that what is legal is therefore right leads to some serious traps. The first pitfall involves a fallacy. It is identified as the *argumentum ad populum*, a fancy way of saying that truth is determined by counting noses (or ballots). This fallacy assumes that if a majority agrees that something is true, then it must be true. This is the type of argument that ancient astronomers forgot to tell Copernicus, Kepler, and Galileo.

Even though people ought not to uncritically accept whatever the government declares is legal, the fact remains that many people do. We cannot, therefore, ignore this as a powerful factor in explaining the massive shift in public opinion on abortion in the past decades.

Ethics, conscience, and abortion

Earlier in United States history, a folk hero who became a congressman wrestled with the problem of making ethical choices. Davy Crockett once declared, "Be sure you're right; then go ahead." This adage is both prudent and dangerous. It is prudent in that it echoes a biblical principle that gives guidance when we lack moral certainty. In his epistle to the Romans, the apostle Paul gave extensive counsel to Christians regarding such matters. The issue was the legality of Christians eating meat that had been offered to idols in pagan rituals. Some believers were convinced such dining was wrong, while others were persuaded it was acceptable. Paul gave this counsel:

> I know and am persuaded in the Lord Jesus that nothing is unclean in itself, but it is unclean for anyone who thinks it unclean. For if your brother is grieved by what you eat, you are no longer walking in love. By what you eat, do not destroy the one for whom Christ died. So do not let what you regard as good be spoken of as evil. For the kingdom of God is not a matter of eating and drinking but of righteousness and peace and joy in the Holy Spirit. Whoever thus serves Christ is acceptable to God

and approved by men. So then let us pursue what makes for peace and for mutual upbuilding.

Do not, for the sake of food, destroy the work of God. Everything is indeed clean, but it is wrong for anyone to make another stumble by what he eats. It is good not to eat meat or drink wine or do anything that causes your brother to stumble. The faith that you have, keep between yourself and God. Blessed is the one who has no reason to pass judgment on himself for what he approves. But whoever has doubts is condemned if he eats, because the eating is not from faith. For whatever does not proceed from faith is sin. (Rom. 14:14–23)

Eating meat offered to idols in itself is not that crucial. It is a matter of ethical indifference, and Christians are free to exercise their Christian liberty in the matter. But it becomes an ethical issue when a person *believes* it is wrong.

What happens if someone performs an action he believes to be wrong, even though it is not in fact wrong? In such a case, Paul judges the action to be wrong. Why? It is wrong because it involves acting in bad faith or against one's conscience. This cardinal principle is found in verse 23: "Whatever does not proceed from faith is sin."

For example, suppose God does not consider dancing a sin, yet I am reared in a subculture that teaches that it is a sin to dance. As a result, I am convinced that dancing is a sin. If I dance while thus convinced, I sin. I am deliberately doing something that I think is contrary to the law of God.

In this case, I am sure I am wrong. On the other hand, if I am sure I am right before I proceed to do something, I am not acting in bad faith. I am doing what I believe is the right thing.

The question remains: If I am not sure I am right, should I go ahead? Davy Crockett seems to say no. Paul's advice is even stronger: If it is not of faith, it is sin.

To be sure, there are occasions when, after careful consideration of ethical principles, we are still not certain what is the proper action. We are out of time or have exhausted our ability for reflection, but we must make a decision and act. Either option before us may be sinful or just—we simply cannot discern which. It is in these excruciating circumstances that we remember the advice of Martin Luther to "sin boldly." Luther meant that if we have done all we can to discern what is right and the time has come to act, then, even if our actions are sinful, we should act with boldness.

How does this concept relate to the question of abortion? If a woman is sure abortion is evil, and it is evil, if she engages in it, she sins. If she is sure that abortion is evil, and it is not evil, if she engages in it, she still sins.

Suppose, however, she is not sure that abortion is evil. Suppose she is uncertain about whether it is a legitimate moral option. Now what does she do? She must first consider her options: abort the fetus or allow it to continue developing. Suppose she sees that there is possible evil in the first option (abortion) and no evil in the second option (proceeding with the pregnancy). Then she has only one legitimate ethical option: to abstain from abortion. Here the uncertainty is in only one direction—abortion. In such cases, the biblical mandate requires us to say no to the uncertain option.

To summarize: If we face two options, one of which clearly is legitimate and one that is possibly but not certainly evil, we must refrain from the second or we inadvertently become guilty of evil. The practical impact of this is clear: Before an abortion is sought, a person must have compelling ethical justification to back it up. Personal preferences, the desire to avoid inconvenience, and the social or legal acceptance of such practices are not biblical warrants for acting without faith. This means that the burden of proof in the abortion debate rests with those who insist that abortion is something God allows. If there is evidence that God might disallow it, we must have strong evidence to the contrary if we are to act in good faith.

In this instance, Crockett's advice is sound: "Be sure you're right; then go ahead." But we must not overlook the expanded application of this maxim: "If you don't know what's right, then don't go ahead, especially if you have another option that is right."

Should conscience be your guide?

What is dangerous about Crockett's advice? If a person is sure he is right, that is no guarantee that he is right. We can sin mightily while thinking we are acting in perfect virtue.

Though it is perilous to act against conscience, we must remember that our consciences are not the final norm by which our ethics are judged. A conscience may be uninformed, seared, dulled, or distorted.

How our consciences are informed is crucial. At the Diet of Worms, Luther was called on by church and state to renounce his views. He declared, "Unless I am convinced by Scripture and plain reason—I do not accept the authority of popes and councils ...my conscience is captive to the Word of God. I cannot ... recant anything, for to go against conscience is neither right nor safe."[49] Luther was saying, "Show me by the teaching of the Bible, or by clear and sound reasoning, or I will not change my position." He was not willing to follow a certain path merely because it was the conventional or socially acceptable path. He sought a clear and certain basis for his conduct.

In every ethical crisis, people argue passionately and eloquently for both sides of the issue. Sometimes the arguments on both sides are more emotional than rational. I went through a major ethical struggle early in my career, when I was a college professor of philosophy. Many of my students were wrestling with their consciences over the rightness or wrongness of serving in the armed forces during the Vietnam War. Some of them turned to me for advice. I was uncertain whether the United States' involvement in Vietnam was just or unjust. I was not a pacifist, but neither was I a warmonger. I believed in the classical just-war theory, which declares that though all wars are evil, not everyone's involvement in war is evil.

Because of my uncertainty about the Vietnam conflict, I read everything I could find and listened to debates to form my conclusions. The debates were emotional and strident, as the nation was divided between hawks and doves. What alarmed me most were the weak and often sloppy arguments used by both sides. The issue was complex, but the public debates were simplistic. I heard hawks say, "My country, right or wrong." This was a ghastly justification for an armed conflict. The doves shouted, "Better Red than dead," a feeble argument for avoiding participation in a just military struggle.

At one symposium, a professor of ethics made an observation that sounded a bit like Crockett's maxim: "Before we ever pick up a weapon to kill another human being, we must be quite sure that we are acting justly." This professor understood that war is a life-and-death matter and is not to be entered into without clear moral justification.

The analogy to the abortion debate is clear. Before we ever pick up any surgical instrument to destroy a developing human fetus, we must be certain we are acting justly.

What does your conscience say about abortion?

At this point I must ask: "What is *your* conscience telling you on abortion? Why do you hold the position you hold? How did you arrive at your conclusions?" Too much is at stake in this issue to approach it without sober thinking and deep reflection.

Luther declared that to act against conscience is neither right nor safe. We have seen why acting against conscience is not right. Why did Luther add that it was not safe? Surely he had a theological consideration in mind. He was a man who harbored a strong fear of divine judgment. Luther believed in God and was persuaded that God would hold him accountable for all of his actions in this life.

The fear of divine judgment governs my actions regarding abortion. As a theologian, I am firmly convinced that God hates abortion and will judge it thoroughly. I also recognize that not everyone shares my view of God's opinions and intentions.

If there is a God, and if we are convinced that the evidence for His existence is compelling, then without question we are accountable to Him for our actions. Before we choose to participate in abortion, we must give serious consideration to what God's views in the matter might be. To ignore this is to ignore the call of conscience and to place ourselves in a perilous position. If an act against conscience is an act against God, then we can easily see how dangerous such an action is.

This book is addressed primarily to those who are not sure about the ethics of abortion. If you remain uncertain, I urge you again not to engage in abortion unless you are absolutely certain for clear and sound reasons (which I'm not aware of) that abortion is an ethically justifiable action. The simple adage of common wisdom applies to you: "When in doubt, don't."

Summary

- Public opinion on the abortion issue has changed in the direction of the pro-choice or pro-abortion positions. The main reason for this is that abortion was legitimized by the *Roe v. Wade* Supreme Court decision.
- The New Testament teaches that conscience must not be violated in making ethical choices.

- Good advice for any ethical choice, but in particular when making a decision about abortion, is this: "When in doubt, don't."

Discussion Questions

1. Why are so many people unsure of their opinion on abortion?
2. How are our views of morality affected by law?
3. What does the apostle Paul mean by "whatever does not proceed from faith is sin"? How would you respond to a Christian woman who said that God was leading her to have an abortion?
4. Why are some people convinced by simplistic slogans? How should we respond to these slogans?
5. How did you reach your conclusions on abortion?
6. How does our understanding of God's justice affect our view of abortion?

Chapter Six

The Role of Government in Abortion

The Constitution is what the judges say it is.
—Charles Evans Hughes

Who's to say religion and politics shouldn't mix?
Whose Bible are they reading anyway?
—Archbishop Desmond Tutu

These questions are at the core of the abortion debate: Is abortion a private ethical issue or does it fall within the scope of government regulation and control? To what extent should the government be involved? How we answer these questions is determined in large measure by how we understand the fundamental role and nature of government.

Closely related to the proper role of government is the increasingly volatile relationship between church and state. Since much of the opposition to legalized abortion comes from the institutional church and its members, the issue of church and state has grown to crisis proportions.

The matter is complicated by the fact that many church members have a theologically oriented concept of the nature and function of government. Since the Bible is not silent, let's examine the biblical and theological understanding of government.

In the fourth century, Aurelius Augustine, bishop of Hippo in North Africa, wrote a classic work that highlighted the conflict between the authorities of this world and the rule of the kingdom of God. In *The City of God*, Augustine described the tension that Christians experience by living within two kingdoms.

Taking his cue from Scripture, Augustine argued that government should not be viewed as a necessary evil but rather as a necessity because of evil. It is because of sin that human beings injure, kill, rob, or violate other human beings in other ways. The role of government, then, is to restrain evil so that human beings can live in peace and safety with each other.

The biblical concept insists that government is ordained and established by God. In God's eyes, government is a gift. Its institution makes life and society possible.

The first manifestation of earthly government is found in the early chapters of Genesis: "He [God] drove the man out, and at the east of the garden of Eden he placed the cherubim and a flaming sword that turned every way to guard the way to the tree of life" (Gen. 3:24).

This verse comes after the biblical narrative that records the fall of man. After Adam and Eve were disobedient and ate fruit from the forbidden tree, they were expelled from the garden of Eden. A sentry was placed at the entrance to the garden to bar any further access to it. The sentry was angelic and heavenly. His weapon was more down to earth. The angelic guard held a flaming sword.

The flaming sword is the first weapon mentioned in Scripture. It was an instrument for enforcement, so here we see the origin of law enforcement. God issued a command that Adam and Eve must leave the garden and not return. He established a guard with the power to ensure that the law was not violated. We might also view this as the first military force instituted by God. The angelic enforcer was given the responsibility to guard the borders of Eden from invasion by unauthorized individuals. The angel represented the government, an institution that was established to enforce the law. By necessity, it was an institution of force.

The power of coercion

Perhaps the most fundamental of all government rights is the just use of force. The entire concept of government could be reduced to legalized or authorized force. In its pristine form, government functions as the legitimate enforcer of law by which society is organized and maintained.

I once had dinner with a well-known United States senator. In the course of our conversation, the senator made a comment that astounded me. He said, "I do not believe that any government ever has the right to coerce any of its citizens to do anything."

I replied, "Do you mean, then, that no government ever has the right to govern?" The senator admitted that he had not considered the foundational reason for which governments exist.

His oversight is not astonishing. We live in an environment where government is an established reality that is exceedingly complex. This is not a period of governmental formation that would call for reflection and discussion about the fundamental role and nature of government. That occurred in the eighteenth century, when governments in the West were going through radical transitions from monarchies to the new models of republics and democracies.

If, as the senator suggested, no government has the right to coerce its citizens to do anything, it follows logically that no government has the right to enforce its laws. Laws are then reduced to suggestions or advice. Without law enforcement, we could violate government legislation recklessly. If we didn't feel like paying taxes, no one could confiscate our money. If we decided to murder someone, no one could forcibly arrest us. In such cases, the government could invite us to attend jail for a season, but the invitation would have an RSVP that we could choose to ignore.

Upon further reflection, the senator realized he had to amend his original statement. He said, "No government ever has the right to coerce its citizens to do anything *unjustly*." With that qualification, he got to the heart of the matter. The legitimacy of law enforcement presupposes that the laws themselves are just. Any unjust use of force is evil. It is a sign of tyranny.

In a democratically oriented society, the potential for tyranny is often overlooked. Because we have free elections, which most obvious tyrannies prohibit, we think we have an absolute safeguard against tyranny. Every black person in the United States knows the folly of that assumption. Alexis de Tocqueville, in evaluating the American "experiment" of democracy, warned of the potential for the tyranny of the majority. A majority can legislate laws as unjust as those announced by a dictator.

A corresponding principle is that a ballot is a bullet. Every time we cast a ballot in favor of a particular piece of legislation, we are choosing a law that will be backed up by all the force government has at its disposal. By law, government has the power and authority to use force to ensure obedience to the law. With every law, someone's freedom is restricted. For a society to be just, its laws must be just. If an unjust law is passed and enforced, anyone who is coerced to comply with the law is a victim of injustice.

If I think of the ballot as a potential bullet, I will be more careful when I vote. The word *vote* comes from the Latin word *votum*, which means "will." When I cast my vote, I express my will. Indeed, if my vote is decisive or a part of the winning majority, then I am not merely expressing my will but imposing my will on others.

Many people think that the vote is merely a means to express personal desires or to seek personal gain, usually at the expense of others. On the contrary, to be ethically scrupulous in the casting of votes, we must vote only for what is just. To vote for a vested interest without just cause is to exercise tyranny.

The obligations of government

If it is the fundamental right of government to rule by force, then it is the fundamental responsibility of government to exercise that rule justly. No government ever has the moral right to be unjust. Consider the most significant biblical teaching on the nature of government, found in Paul's epistle to the Romans:

> Let every person be subject to the governing authorities. For there is no authority except from God, and those that exist have been instituted by God. Therefore whoever resists the authorities resists what God has appointed, and those who resist will incur judgment. For rulers are not a terror to good conduct, but to bad. Would you have no fear of the one who is in authority? Then do what is good, and you will receive his approval, for he is God's servant for your good. But if you do wrong, be afraid, for he does not bear the sword in vain. For he is the servant of God, an avenger who carries out God's wrath on the wrongdoer. Therefore one must be in subjection, not only to avoid God's wrath but also for the sake of conscience. For because of this you also pay taxes, for the authorities are ministers of God, attending to this very thing. Pay to all what is owed to them: taxes to whom taxes are owed, revenue to whom revenue is owed, respect to whom respect is owed, honor to whom honor is owed.
>
> Owe no one anything, except to love each other, for

the one who loves another has fulfilled the law. For the commandments, "You shall not commit adultery, You shall not murder, You shall not steal, You shall not covet," and any other commandment, are summed up in this word: "You shall love your neighbor as yourself." Love does no wrong to a neighbor; therefore love is the fulfilling of the law. (Rom. 13:1–10)

This passage begins with a command of obedience to civil government. Though the Christian's highest obligation and devotion is directed to God Himself, the Supreme Magistrate, the Supreme Authority, indeed the Author of all authority, commands him to be subject to civil authority. The Bible does not support the attitude that declares, "I will obey God and ignore the state." Christians have a sober mandate to bend over backward to be civilly obedient. (Of course, Christians not only may but must exercise civil disobedience if the civil magistrate commands what God forbids or forbids what God commands.)

The reason Paul gives for his exhortation to obey civil authority is that the authority and power of the state rest in the authority and power of God. Government exists by divine institution; earthly government was ordained by God. To oppose government per se is to oppose God.

The fact that government is instituted by God does not mean that every government is pleasing to God. Like individuals, governments can rebel against God and become instruments of evil. It is ironic that Paul is writing to Christians living in Rome, telling them to be obedient citizens, as it was the government of the

Roman Empire that later unjustly executed the apostle himself.

Government is to be on the side of good and not evil. Since government is instituted by God and is answerable and accountable to Him, it always has the responsibility to act justly. When a government acts unjustly, it becomes a terror to the good, and those who pursue virtue have every reason to fear its awful power.

Even in the corruption of Rome, there was some commitment to justice and virtue. As a general truth, people who were just and virtuous were considered praiseworthy by the Roman state. For example, Rome did not punish businessmen who used honest weights and measures and fulfilled their contracts. To the extent that Rome's system was just, it had the approval of God.

Paul refers to government authorities as servants of God, or ministers. It may seem strange to think of politicians as "ministers," yet the English language still carries that idea. For example, the leading elected official in Great Britain and many other nations is called the "prime minister." Even American politicians describe themselves as "public servants." Elected officials are to serve and minister to the people they represent. In a certain sense, Paul views them as "ordained ministers."

Romans 13:4 declares that the civil magistrate "does not bear the sword in vain." As in the case of Genesis 3, we see that part of the role of government is to use force to maintain the law. In Romans 13, as in Genesis, the sword is the sign of the authorized power of enforcement. The government's power to use the sword is not just symbolic, it is real. The state has nothing less than capital authority.

Paul explains why we are to pay taxes: The government must have funds in order to perform its legitimate tasks. The Christian is commanded not only to pay taxes but also to give the state honor. On several occasions, the Bible requires that Christians pray for those in governing positions.

The latter verses of this passage—involving commands against such things as adultery—may indicate a change in subject by the apostle. I have included them because of the accent given to love, particularly to the love of one's neighbors. Paul does not necessarily change his focus, but merely extends his discussion of the role of government into the realm of the law of love. He says in verse 10 that love is the fulfillment of the law.

The relationship of love and law is connected to our understanding of government. Government is instituted by God as an expression of His love for us, an expression of His grace and mercy toward sinful humanity. When Augustine said that government is necessary because of evil, he obviously understood that what drives the necessity of government is love. If God loves us and we love our fellow men, we will want to see justice established. Injustice is opposed to love; injustice violates love.

The most fundamental expression of love is care for, concern for, and protection of human life. The foundational obligation of all government is to protect, sustain, and maintain human life. This is the very reason for the existence of government.

The scope or sphere of government involvement and enterprise is a matter of perennial debate. Should the government be in the business of delivering mail? Should the government subsidize private businesses? Should it bail out financial institutions, create stimulus packages for consumers, or salvage insolvent mortgages? There is one nonnegotiable issue, though, regarding government involvement: Government must be involved in protecting people from murder. The protection of human life is at the heart of the role of government.

Separation of church and state

Since the Supreme Court decisions of *Roe v. Wade* and *Brown v. Board of Education*, the debate over the separation of church and state has escalated. Legal battles have been fought about teaching creation in public schools, displaying Christmas symbols in public buildings, praying before football games, and a host of other church-state issues. Certainly the protests of religious institutions and religious people against the legalization of abortion have fanned the flames of this controversy.

The separation of church and state does not necessarily mean the separation of the state and God. Though the founding fathers of the United States were not all Christians, they did acknowledge the existence of God. Neither the Declaration of Independence nor the Constitution claims autonomy or ultimate sovereignty for the state. The foundational premise of American government is that the state receives its right to govern from the Creator. The United States was rightly conceived as a nation under God, not over God or independent of God. To acknowledge the existence of a Creator God is to implicitly acknowledge His sovereign authority and ownership over all He creates. To be under God is to be under His authority and power.

Though the United States puts "In God We Trust" on its currency, it is committed by law to refrain from establishing any particular religion. We have no state church in the United States. This is spelled out in the First Amendment to the Constitution: "Congress shall make no law respecting an establishment of religion, or prohibiting the free exercise thereof; or abridging the freedom of speech or of the press, or the right of the people peaceably to assemble and to petition the Government for a redress of grievances."

This provision prohibits the state from exalting a particular religion to a privileged or favored status. If a building funded by public tax dollars is used to promote Christianity, a Jew, a Muslim, or anyone else has the right to cry foul. At the same time, the law guarantees the free exercise of religion. This applies to any and all religions.

Basically, the separation of church and state means that these two institutions perform distinct and separate functions. It is not the task of the church to provide for the national defense or to bear arms. Conversely, it is not the task of the state to administer the sacraments or to preach the gospel. Each institution has a distinctive role to play. Ideally these roles are to be carried out with mutual respect and cooperation. The state is to ensure that the church has the freedom to carry out its mission, and the church is to be supportive of the state in carrying out its mission. This separation was never intended to devolve into a rivalry for power and control.

There are times when the two institutions must interact. For example, if the church is guilty of misappropriation of funds, the state has a right and a duty to become involved. Likewise, if the state becomes involved in unjust actions, the church has a right and a duty to exercise prophetic criticism toward the state.

Any adherent of a religious institution is involved in both spheres. Because a person is a Christian, a Jew, or a Muslim, he or she is not automatically disfranchised from the state. Indeed, even if a person is ordained clergy, he is still able to run for public office. However, a religious person does not have the moral right to use the political arena for vested interests if those interests are unjust.

What is an appropriate role, then, for people and churches that wish to contest abortion laws? When the church calls on the state to prohibit abortion, the state is not being asked to establish a religion. Nor is the state being asked to be the church. The church is simply asking the state to be the state. If it is the role of the state to protect, sustain, and maintain human life, and if it is the conviction of the church that abortion involves the destruction of human life, then it follows that the church has the right to call the state to outlaw abortion. The church is not asking the state to baptize human beings, but to protect the lives of unborn humans.

From a theological perspective, abortion is a "common grace" issue; that is, it involves the common welfare of humanity. When the church encourages the state to aid those suffering from a natural disaster such as a hurricane or an earthquake, the church is asking the state to assist in the common cause of meeting human need. Though Christians and churches may at times overstep the boundaries and improperly intrude their religious concerns into the public sphere, I do not think this is the case with abortion. There is no greater arena of common grace and common concern than human life.

It is clear that abortion is considered by many to be only a moral issue. This has led to the prevalent opinion that opposition to abortion involves an unwarranted intrusion of the church into the public domain.

The legislating of morality

A frequently heard slogan is, "You can't legislate morality." This phrase has undergone a strange evolution in meaning. The expression originally meant a person's behavior cannot automatically be altered by simply passing laws; legislation doesn't stop people from doing what they are determined to do. However, the contemporary meaning of the phrase is that it is wrong or illegitimate to enact legislation that restricts moral behavior.

This is a ridiculous notion. If it were applied consistently, the government would enact very little legislation. Perhaps Congress could spend its time debating the colors of the flag or naming an official national bird. Virtually all government legislation has moral ramifications. It is a moral question whether people are permitted to steal the private property of others. Murder is a moral matter. How one drives a car on the highway has moral implications, because reckless driving represents a clear and present danger to the welfare of other people. Ecological considerations in legislation have moral import. The list could continue almost indefinitely. To argue that the state should not legislate moral behavior is silly and thoughtless.

Perhaps the intent of "you can't legislate morality" is that the state should not interfere in matters of private morality as distinguished from public morality. We hear strident appeals that government should ignore the private behavior of consenting adults. However, the moment the consenting adults involve someone else, the matter is no longer private but by definition social. Since the question of abortion involves at the very least the destiny of a potential human being other than the consenting adults, it is a societal and public matter.

A fundamental concern of law is the protection of the weak against the strong and powerful. Such weakness is vividly seen in the utter helplessness of the unborn baby. The unborn have no voting rights and no physical power to avert their destruction. If their interests are to be served and protected, it must be by adults in general and by government in particular. The Supreme Court decided that the state has no compelling interest in the fetus until viability. (One wonders at what point the fetus has a compelling interest in the state.) By denying the unborn the fundamental right to live, the state has reneged on its solemn duty.

The *Roe v. Wade* decision has provoked the most serious ethical crisis in the history of the United States. This is the nadir in American jurisprudence, the moment of the state's greatest failure to be the state.

Summary

- Government is a divine gift. Its role is to restrain evil so that human beings can live in peace and safety.
- The most fundamental right of government is the just use of force.
- According to Scripture, the authority and power of the state rest in the authority and power of God.
- The protection of human life is at the head of proper governmental concern.
- The foundational premise of the United States government is that the state receives the right to govern from the Creator.
- Separation of church and state means that the two entities perform distinct and separate functions. The separation does not necessarily mean the separation of the state and God.
- Because moral issues are at the center of all human endeavors, government inevitably is involved in "legislating morality."

Discussion Questions

1. Why do some in society think that the church should not speak out on political issues? Why do some in the church think that the church should avoid political or legislative affairs?

2. What is the state's responsibility in the abortion debate? What is the church's responsibility?

3. What do you fear most when you or your church become involved in governmental or legislative affairs?

4. When must Christians disobey the governing authorities?

5. What is the best possible relationship between church and state?

6. Is abortion a matter of private morality? Why or why not?

Part II

AN ANALYSIS OF
PRO-ABORTION AND
PRO-CHOICE ARGUMENTS

Chapter Seven

A Woman's Right to Her Body

*Every man . . . is an end in himself, he exists for his own sake, and
the achievement of his own happiness is his highest moral purpose.*
—Ayn Rand

*Feminists need to ask why the "sexist" establishment supports
abortion. It may be that abortion enhances the male's freedom
to exploit by sparing him from the worry of paternity.*
—Bill Crouse

One of the most frequent arguments heard in favor of legal abortion is that a woman has a right to her body. What does this mean?

The current debate is not over whether or not a woman in the United States has the legal right to her body with respect to abortion. Since the *Roe v. Wade* decision, she has that right. But *should* she have that right?

The right to privacy

The closest the Constitution comes to affirming a woman's right to her body is an implied "right to privacy." *Roe v. Wade* utilized the Ninth and Fourteenth Amendments to make this claim. Among abortion adherents, there is a strong sentiment that abortion legislation improperly intrudes into the privacy rights of people and families. In simple language, they plead that it is none of the state's business whether a woman terminates her pregnancy or chooses to carry it to term.

The relevant portions of the United States Constitution are as follows:

> The enumeration in the Constitution of certain rights shall not be construed to deny or disparage others retained by the people. (Ninth Amendment, 1791)

> Section 1. All persons born or naturalized in the United States and subject to the jurisdiction thereof, are citizens of the United States and of the State wherein they reside. No State shall make or enforce any law which shall abridge the privileges or immunities of citizens of the United States; nor shall any State deprive any person of life, liberty, or property, without due process of law; nor deny to any person within its jurisdiction the equal protection of the laws. (Fourteenth Amendment, 1868)

Immediately evident from even a cursory reading of these amendments is the absence of a single explicit word about privacy rights. The concept of the right to privacy, on which legalized abortion is based, is not mentioned explicitly anywhere in the Constitution. Without analysis, the majority opinion in *Roe v. Wade* decided the issue by simple assertion: "This right of privacy, whether it be founded in the Fourteenth Amendment's concept of personal liberty and restrictions upon state action, as we feel it is, or, as the District Court determined, in the Ninth Amendment's reservation of rights to the people, is broad enough to encompass a woman's decision whether or not to terminate her pregnancy."[50]

The Supreme Court should not be faulted for being jealous to protect the privacy rights of citizens from the unwarranted invasion or intrusion of the state. Few of us have a desire to live with Big Brother monitoring our every action and eavesdropping on our every word. The specter of such a society is hideous. We should be thankful we have such things as locks for our bedroom doors. But this question remains: Is there any ethical or moral justification for including the right to have an abortion under the broader category of the right to privacy?

From an ethical perspective, we must raise this question: Is the right to privacy an absolute right? Does God, for example, give us the right to blaspheme Him as long as we don't do it publicly? Do I have the right to murder someone or disfigure his property as long as I do it in privacy? Obviously not. There are moral limitations to the right of privacy. How far do those limitations extend?

Once again, the debate returns to the question of when life begins. If the justices of the Supreme Court had been convinced that the fetus is a living human person, it is highly unlikely that they would have included destroying the fetus within the right to privacy. Surely the right to privacy is not a higher or greater right than the right to life. If it were, I would have the moral right to take the life of anyone who invaded my privacy.

Because I speak nationally and have a national radio ministry, I have experienced a substantive loss of privacy. Though I am not hounded like movie stars or famous athletes, nevertheless I know what it means to have my dinner interrupted in a restaurant by someone who wants me to autograph a book. These interruptions are infrequent and mild, but real nevertheless. Any person who works in the public eye knows some sense of the loss of privacy. We rarely understand how important privacy is until we lose some of it.

We can understand a celebrity's annoyance when he or she is disturbed in a public place, but we would hardly argue that in such instances the celebrity has the right to kill the fan or the news reporter. We understand that the right to life transcends the right to privacy. If a fetus is a human life, then the Supreme Court erred in allowing the destruction of the fetus under the application of the right of privacy.

A woman's moral rights to her body

Most people agree that a woman certainly has a considerable number of rights to her body. She has a right not to be subjected to rape or malicious physical injury, for example. But is the woman's right to her body absolute? In addition to the legal right related to abortion, does a woman have the moral right to do anything she pleases with her body? For example, can a woman use her body as a battering ram to injure others? Does she have a moral right to sell her body in prostitution? Is she free to mutilate her body or to destroy it through suicide? These questions reveal that the issue of a woman's right to her body is more complicated than it first appears.

Whatever moral rights a woman has to her body must be grounded in some norm; otherwise, the claim is arbitrary. From where does a moral right to one's body with respect to abortion come? Is it given by God? That would be exceedingly difficult to prove. Does it come from some other ethical norm? If so, which one?

A woman does have some rights to her body. However, it is not evident that she has an *absolute* right to her body. The right to abortion, based on the right to one's body, demands justification beyond mere assertion.

Is the fetus a part of the woman's body?

Contained within the argument concerning the rights a woman has to her body is an assumption that must be challenged—that the fetus is a part of the woman's body. The fetus is contained within the woman's body and is connected to it, but that does not mean the fetus is a part of the mother's body. It is more accurate to say that though the fetus shares the same geographical location of the woman's body, the fetus is not *essentially* a part of her body. We can distinguish between the essence of the woman's body and the essence of the fetus. Given the gestation process, the fetus is neither the product essentially or organically of the mother's body alone, nor is the fetus a permanent fixture of the woman's body. Left to the natural course, the unborn baby will leave the mother's body to carry out his or her own life. As such, the fetus is capable of being essentially distinct from the essence of the mother. The fetus has a brain, a heart, and fingerprints—a unique identity, which is not merely personal but is also physical. The biological structure and essence of the fetus is not exactly the same as the biological structure and essence of the mother.

The discovery of genetic fingerprinting added important information to this discussion. In the early 1980s, a British geneticist named Alec Jeffries made a surprising discovery in the process of mapping human genes. Jeffries extracted DNA molecules from a sample of blood cells and cut them into unequal bits by adding enzymes. The fragments were put into a gel, where an electrical field caused the larger fragments to separate from the smaller ones. The DNA fragment pattern was transferred to a nylon membrane. Jeffries then added radioactively labeled pieces of DNA to act as probes. The membrane was then subjected to X-ray analysis. The X-ray film revealed vast numbers of genetic markers that exhibited an amazing degree of individual specificity.

Later experiments—both in England and in the United States—confirmed that each person, with the exception of identical twins, has a unique genetic fingerprint. In 1985, Jeffries declared: "You would have to look for one part in a million million million million million before you would find one pair with the same genetic fingerprint, and with the world population of only five billion it can be categorically said that a genetic fingerprint is individually specific and that any pattern, excepting identical twins, does not belong to anyone on the face of this planet whoever has been or ever will be."[51]

If any single cell of a woman's body is analyzed to find its essential biological structure, each and every cell will have the same genetic fingerprint. Likewise, an analysis of the cells of the fetus will determine that each cell has the same genetic fingerprint—which is different from that of the mother. This indicates that, at the physical biological level, there is a clear line of demarcation between the body of the fetus and the body of the mother. Two distinct sets of human tissue reside in the pregnant woman's body.

How about the father? Does he have any rights related to the fetus? Although the father does not carry the fetus in his body, he has contributed half of the substance that is the genetic structure of the fetus. In the case of abortion, at least three people (not to mention grandparents and other ancestors who contributed to the unique genetic structure of the fetus) have a stake in the woman's decision about "her body."

Without a solid justification, is the argument for the right to one's body just another way of obtaining personal preference? The least charitable interpretation is to say it is a thinly veiled tactic to earn the right to do what one wants.

I do not want to imply that selfishness is the only reason

behind the argument for a woman's right to her body. It is important, however, that those who advance this argument be careful
to clarify their precise meaning. Because of the various possible
interpretations and their inherent weaknesses, the argument, as
it is so frequently and simply stated, is insufficient ground for
justifying abortion.

Summary

- Women were granted the legal right to their bodies
  as it relates to abortion by the *Roe v. Wade* Supreme
  Court decision. The court ruled that this right was
  implied by the Constitution's Ninth and Fourteenth
  amendments.
- The right to life transcends the right to privacy.
- No people, including women, have an absolute right
  to do anything they wish with their bodies.
- The fetus, although sharing geographical space
  within a woman's body and connected to her, has a
  distinct genetic imprint and in essence is a separate
  entity, not a part of the woman's body.

Discussion Questions

1. Why is it seemingly so easy for people to get away
   with invalid arguments in the mass media? Why do
   many people so easily miss the logical fallacies in
   invalid arguments?

2. What restraints are placed on our rights to our bodies (see 1 Cor. 6:9–10)?

3. What kind of right do most people mean by a "right to one's body"? Where does this right come from?

4. Is the fetus a part of the woman's body? Why or why not?

5. Do we have any right to privacy? How would you frame that right if you were writing a constitution?

6. How does a woman have a right to choose regarding pregnancy?

Chapter Eight

Three Frequent Assertions

Duty is ours; consequences are God's.
—Gen. Thomas "Stonewall" Jackson

Men no longer are bound together by ideas, but by interest.
—Alexis de Tocqueville

Pro-abortion and pro-choice activists often rely on three basic arguments:

• If abortion is made illegal, women will have dangerous back-alley abortions.

• It is inconsistent to be anti-abortion and pro-capital punishment.

• Men should not speak about abortion because it is a women's issue.

Each of these arguments can be answered without hesitation or apology.

If abortion is made illegal, women will have dangerous back-alley abortions

Pro-abortion activists predict there will be a carnage of human life if existing abortion laws are changed. How valid is this argument, which is based ultimately on the "lesser of two evils" principle? The thinking is that though legal abortion may not be entirely desirable, it is more desirable than the alternative. If abortion is outlawed, it is said, women will be forced to place their lives in the hands of unskilled and unscrupulous back-alley butchers.

This argument assumes that if abortion is made illegal a significant number of women will still have them. Instead of being performed by qualified physicians in antiseptic environments, abortions will be performed in dingy criminal settings or by rank amateurs armed with coat hangers. Though this scenario may seem overly dramatic, it does have historical precedent and is therefore realistic.

The argument rests on a fairly sound premise. In all likelihood, if the law prohibited abortion, some women would still seek them and might even have them in perilous circumstances. Some women would become the victims of gynecological butchery. This is no small horror to contemplate.

More women have died from abortions in the United States since abortion was legalized than in the preceding times of illegal abortion. This is due not to the incompetence of the physicians but to the huge increase in the number of abortions performed. Pro-life activists tend to assume that if abortion is once again made illegal, the number of women who die or are permanently injured from abortions will dramatically decrease to pre-*Roe v. Wade* levels. This assumption probably makes an enormous leap of faith. If *Roe v. Wade* were reversed, it is highly unlikely that the number of deaths would revert to what it was before.

Our culture has gone through nearly four decades of legal abortion. Now it is a widely accepted practice, and the strong social taboos that exercised restraint on abortion prior to *Roe v. Wade* will probably not make a swift or certain comeback. Whether we like it or not, abortion on demand is part of the fabric of current experience. Here we see evidence of the original meaning of "you can't legislate morality." This makes the practical consequences of the reversal of abortion law a very serious matter. Whether abortion remains legal or is made illegal, women are going to continue to have abortions—and, as a result, risk death.

The ethical issue at stake, however, is not only the women who are dying or who may die, but also the unborn babies who are killed every year—one and a half million in the United States alone. This remains the focal point of the debate. For those convinced that abortion involves killing living human beings, the continuation of it to protect those who are having the abortions is ethically intolerable. The loss of a woman's life in abortion is a tragic thing; but if abortion is evil, then the life lost is that of the guilty party. The destruction of the unborn baby is the loss of the innocent party. Ideally, we should refrain from abortion altogether, because then neither the woman nor the baby would die.

If the practice of abortion is unjust, then the protection of those who engage in the practice is not the duty of the state. Concern for them is certainly the duty of the church, but to protect a criminal in the course of committing a crime is not the responsibility of government.

Again, the argument based on the concern for the harm that will come to women who have illegal abortions presumes that aborting unborn babies is a legitimate practice. In all likelihood, if the pro-abortion activist who uses this argument were to be convinced that the unborn are living human beings, this argument from practical expediency would vanish in view of the greater evil of the destruction of babies.

It is inconsistent to be anti-abortion and pro-capital punishment

Pro-abortion activists repeatedly have charged pro-life activists with a hypocritical inconsistency. The argument is that if pro-life activists are so stirred up about the loss of the life of unborn babies, why are they not equally concerned about the fate of men and women who are executed by the criminal justice system? Even talk show host Larry King made this charge, saying that he would give no credence to pro-life supporters until they became more consistent in their two positions.

There are two responses. The first has to do with the logic of King's complaint. Even if pro-life activists are wrong about their view of capital punishment and are utterly inconsistent in their views on the two matters, that does not disqualify their grounds for objection to abortion. A person may hold inconsistent views on two subjects and still be correct on one of them. King must allow logically for the possibility of the happy inconsistency. No one is right in all of his or her thinking, and each person has some points of inconsistency. That does not invalidate everything we believe.

Second, are anti-abortion and pro-capital punishment views in fact inconsistent? The biblical view of the overarching sanctity of life is the same principle that leads people to be both anti-abortion and pro-capital punishment. The biblical reason for the institution of capital punishment is that murder is an intolerable violation of the sanctity of life. The murderer who willfully and maliciously takes a life thereby forfeits his right to his own life.

Whether King or others agree with this position, its weakness is not one of inconsistency. Advocates of capital punishment cannot rightly be charged with espousing a principle of injustice. If a murderer is killed as a penalty for killing someone else, the punishment is perfectly just. The penalty may not be merciful, but it is not unjust. An injustice would be done to the murderer only if his penalty were more severe than his crime.

Men should not speak about abortion because it is a women's issue

It is a specious argument to say that men should not speak about abortion because it is a women's issue. Some people include it as an extension of the argument for a woman's right to privacy. That is, since childbearing is exclusive to women, men have no right to address moral issues connected to it. Such statements as, "If men had to carry babies in pregnancy, there would be no laws against abortion," reflect this radical view.

I once received a letter from a Christian woman who chided me on precisely this point. She maintained that I had no right to speak or write on abortion because I am a man. Since she was a professing Christian, I wondered what she would say if the Lord Jesus Christ were to appear and begin speaking about abortion. Would she disqualify Him as well simply on the basis that He is male?

This argument is a crass form of reverse sexism and female chauvinism. It is unworthy of the feminist position, slanderous to men, and trivial in its conception. If we followed this principle to its logical conclusion, we would have to dismiss Moses, Paul, Socrates, Plato, Confucius, or any other male teacher of ethics from the discussion. Ultimately, we would have to disqualify seven of nine of the current justices of the Supreme Court, leaving Justices Ruth Bader Ginsburg and Sonia Sotomayor to decide the matter by themselves.

More soberly, it is important to realize that the current division over abortion is not simply a division between men and women. Women are at the forefront of the pro-life movement, and countless men are involved in the pro-choice ranks. A common tactic in debate or discussion is to attack the soundness of an argument by attacking the person who espouses it. If abortion is just, then it doesn't matter who argues for it—male or female, black or white, Asian or European. The argument must be decided on its own merits, not on the personalities involved.

Summary

- It is likely that abortion will continue to be in high demand even if it becomes illegal.
- Although the death of a woman in any abortion—legal or illegal—is tragic, the focal point of the abortion debate must remain the unborn child.
- Anti-abortion and pro-capital punishment views are not biblically inconsistent. A high view of the sanctity of life is foundational to both positions.
- Abortion is not just a women's issue. Since the father contributes one-half of the genetic structure of the fetus, men should be involved in the abortion discussion.

Discussion Questions

1. Is legalized abortion the lesser of two evils?
2. What unspoken assumptions are part of the "back-alley abortion" arguments?
3. If abortion were illegal, what could be done to minimize the number of illegal abortions?
4. What is the government's responsibility concerning the safety of lawbreakers?

5. Must those who are pro-life be against capital punishment in order to be consistent?

6. If men were disallowed from dealing with the abortion issue, what issue would that exclude women from?

7. How can pro-life activists exhibit an image of consistent reasoning and concern?

Chapter Nine

The Pro-Choice Position

If we don't know, then shouldn't we morally opt on the side
that is life? If you came upon an immobile body and you
yourself could not determine whether it was dead or alive,
I think that you would decide to consider it alive until
someone could prove it was dead. You wouldn't get a shovel
and start covering it up. And I think we should do
the same thing with regard to abortion.
—President Ronald Reagan

In the ongoing debate about abortion, the pro-choice position has become pivotal to public opinion. Over the past four decades, poll after poll has shown that anywhere from half to three-fourths of all Americans agreed with this statement: "I personally feel that abortion is morally wrong, but I also feel that the decision as to whether to have an abortion has to be made by every woman herself."

Why is the pro-choice position so attractive and vigorously guarded? To learn why, it is important first to review the historical strategy of the militant pro-abortion groups.

In the early 1970s, prior to *Roe v. Wade*, militant advocates of legalized abortion met to plan and adopt a strategy for changing the abortion climate in the United States. Their strategy later was made public by defectors whose thinking on abortion changed. Dr. Bernard Nathanson, a physician who performed thousands of legal abortions before he became utterly convinced that he was destroying human life, made public the initial pro-abortion plan.

The strategy was as old as it was effective—the classic "divide and conquer" plan. First the pro-abortion activists asked themselves, "From where will the fiercest opposition to abortion come?" They rightly concluded it would be from the Roman Catholic Church. In order to counterbalance this powerful influence, they sought to enlist the support of mainline Protestant denominations. Pro-abortion activists did not ask these denominations to openly endorse the pro-abortion position; rather, they suggested a less-offensive middle-ground position called "pro-choice." They appealed to a sense of fair play in overcoming what they perceived as tyranny emanating from Rome.

At this same time, many of the mainline churches were involved in controversies on vital issues relating to feminism. The barriers against the ordination of women were crumbling, and women had won unprecedented positions of church authority and power. These sweeping gains had been won at painful cost, but many women were fearful that their gains were not secure. By linking the pro-choice position to that of women's rights, the pro-abortion activists' strategy was effective in gaining wide-spread endorsement for the pro-choice cause from Protestant denominations. In a vital sense, the pro-choice position rode the coattails of the women's-rights position in the churches. Those who were struggling for the consolidation of women's rights in the church perceived that adopting the pro-choice position was critical, or their activism for other rights might be weakened.

Outside the church, the secular public was encouraged to adopt pro-choice views because of the link to feminism and the cherished principle of freedom of choice. Freedom of choice is as American as baseball and apple pie.

The emphasis of the pro-abortion strategy was not to convert people to a clear position in favor of abortion, but merely to get them to affirm each person's inalienable right to choose without government intervention or coercion. This was a standard statement: "I'm personally not in favor of abortion, but I don't want to impose my view on others. It's a matter of individual liberty and private conscience."

While the pro-abortion strategy focused attention on women's dignity and rights, individual liberty, private matters of conscience, and the freedom of the state to ignore the church's morality, the cardinal issue of abortion—the rights of the unborn—receded into the background, slowly obscured by side issues.

Legal allies: pro-abortion and pro-choice positions

What the pro-abortion strategists clearly understood was not so clearly perceived by those standing on the "middle ground" of the pro-choice position. The pro-choice position may seem safe culturally, socially, and ethically, but it is not a middle ground on the legal front. This was the brilliance of the pro-abortion strategy: From a legal perspective, a vote for choice is a vote for abortion. The difference between the two positions is inconsequential, and legally, they are allies in the same camp.

This is so because the present laws do not mandate abortion; they *allow* it. As long as the law does not prohibit abortion, it serves the cause of both the pro-abortion and pro-choice camps. When individuals vote "pro-choice," they vote to allow abortion, which is the exact goal of the militant pro-abortionist.

The pro-abortion activists parlayed their small number into a national majority of public opinion by gaining the silent majority as their ally. Although the pro-abortion activists were (and are) far outnumbered by the anti-abortion, pro-life activists, they were able to swell their ranks dramatically by gathering all who are pro-choice. A significant shift occurred in the terminology used in the debate: Pro-abortion activists adopted the label of pro-choice for themselves. Time will tell whether this will provoke a backlash from the middle-of-the-road pro-choice activists, who may rebel if the pro-choice position becomes clearly identified with pro-abortion. Indeed, recent debates over health-care reform and taxpayer subsidies for abortion have already begun to erode the pro-choice/pro-abortion coalition.

A person who is conscientiously pro-choice must understand that he or she is a legal ally, willingly or unwillingly, with the pro-abortion position. If you the reader have taken a pro-choice position to avoid either extreme camp, you must squarely face the reality that from a legal standpoint you have chosen the pro-abortion camp.

The meaning of pro-choice

What is the substance of the pro-choice position? If a woman says that she personally would not have an abortion but does not want to deny someone else's right to do it, on what grounds would this woman hesitate to get an abortion? Perhaps she simply wants to have as many babies as possible and doesn't anticipate ever facing an unwanted pregnancy. Maybe this person thinks a fetus is a living human being or is not sure about the fetus' status. Perhaps she believes that the fetus is a living human being but does not want to impose this view on others. Here we reach the crux of the pro-choice position. Is the right to choose an absolute right? Do we have the moral right to choose what is morally wrong? To ask such a question is to answer it.

Again, every law enacted limits or restricts someone's choices. That is the very nature of law. If we do not wish to restrict other people's choices through legislation, we must stop legislating and cease voting. I think that most people will grant that freedom of choice is not an absolute freedom. No human being is an absolute law unto himself. Unless we are prepared to buy into an ethical system of pure relativism by which law and society become impossible, we must flee as the wind from the proposition that the individual is autonomous.

To move from the abstract into the concrete, I wonder whether pro-choice activists object to laws protecting their personal property rights? Does the thief breaking into a home to steal someone's television have the inalienable right to make that choice? Does a man have the right to choose to rape a woman? These extreme examples make it obvious that freedom of choice cannot be considered an absolute right.

At what line must freedom of choice end? I believe it ends where my freedom of choice steps on another person's inalienable rights of life and liberty. No unborn baby has ever had the right to choose or deny its own destruction. Indeed, as others have said, the most dangerous place in the United States for a human being is inside the womb of a woman. For millions of unborn babies, the womb has become a cell on death row. The inmate is summarily executed without benefit of a trial or a word of defense. This execution literally involves being torn limb from limb. Is this description too graphic? Is it too emotionally provocative? No. It would be only if the description were untrue.

The right to choose, as sacred as it may be, does not carry with it the arbitrary right to destroy a human life. This is as much a miscarriage of justice as it is a miscarriage of a human baby.

What is it about the freedom to choose that makes it so precious? What provoked Patrick Henry to cry, "Give me liberty or give me death"? Certainly we desire some self-determination, and the idea of living under external coercion is abhorrent. We are thinking creatures, and we value our freedom to make choices. Most of us would hate being imprisoned, but even in a maximum-security penitentiary, a person's right to choose is not totally stripped away.

It is this principle of self-determination—having a say in

my own condition and future—that is brutally denied to every unborn, aborted child. I had no say in my mother's decision whether to have an abortion or to carry me to term. My entire life was in her hands. Had she chosen abortion, my life would have been snuffed out before I was born. You and I are real human beings. We were once helpless to exercise our own precious right to choose. We were once totally dependent on somebody else's choice for our very existence.

A second crucial dimension of the right to choose is the question of when to make the moral choice concerning the baby's life. (Because this involves sexual morality, it is a very unpopular subject in the discussion.) The time to choose whether or not to have a baby is not *after* the baby has been conceived and begun its development. Except in cases of rape, sexual intercourse with or without means of contraception is still a matter of choice. Choices we make, whether of a sexual or nonsexual nature, always have consequences. It is an axiom of ethics and of law that we are responsible for the consequences of our choices.

When we have sexual intercourse, we may not intend or desire to produce another human life. We are aware, however, that intercourse begins the reproduction process and can produce such offspring. To kill the offspring is hardly a responsible or moral method of handling this decision.

Pro-choice and women's-rights positions

The close link historically between the pro-choice and women's-rights positions already has been explained. To be anti-abortion does not equal being anti-women. On the contrary, I am persuaded that being pro-life equals being radically pro-women. Women have value and dignity because of their basic humanity, not because of their gender. A vote for abortion is a vote against the sanctity of life—the sanctity of female life as well as the sanctity of male life. Abortion is not a gender issue, it is a human life issue.

The feminist movement is driven by the relentless pursuit of human dignity. That is why it seems a radical distortion and gross inconsistency to link feminism with the pro-abortion or pro-choice positions. The pro-abortion and pro-choice positions do little for the cause of human dignity. On the contrary, they demean human dignity and, by implication, the dignity of women.

Are you pro-choice or undecided?

In conclusion, if a woman avoids abortion personally because she is convinced abortion takes a human life, but she does not want to violate someone else's right to choose, she has made the fatal ethical error of promoting the right to choose above the more fundamental right to life. If I lose my right to live, my right to choose becomes moot. The right to choose is grounded on the right to life. Therefore, I urge you, if you hold the pro-choice position on these grounds, to change your vote to pro-life.

I recognize, however, that many who are pro-choice are basically uncertain. This is primarily why I have written this book. My purpose has been to convince the undecided that the pro-life view is the proper ethical option. I believe the evidence is overwhelming that an embryo or fetus is a living human being.

However, even after weighing the evidence, some of you will wonder whether a fetus is a living human being. If that describes you, I urge you to review chapter 5 on what to do in the case of moral or ethical uncertainty. It is understandable that if you are unsure of your own opinion, you would be reluctant to impose that view on others.

I must state again forcefully that the pro-choice view is not an undecided or middle-ground position. It supports the view that freedom of choice includes the freedom to choose an abortion. It lands on the "pro" rather than the "con" side of the abortion issue.

Are you inclined to the pro-choice position on the grounds of moral uncertainty? I believe you have another alternative, one that will remove you from an ethically questionable position. Why not simply declare that you are undecided? To be undecided is to not opt for the pro-abortion, pro-life, or pro-choice positions.

Summary

- The current abortion situation in the United States is to some extent the result of a carefully planned and executed strategy of pro-abortion groups.
- The "pro-choice" middle-ground alternative is a pro-abortion position from a legal perspective.
- The right to choose is not an absolute right that outweighs the more fundamental right to life.
- The legitimate moral and ethical choice as to whether or not to produce or prevent human life is made prior to sexual intercourse.

- For those who are uncomfortable with the pro-life, pro-abortion, or pro-choice positions, there is another possibility: undecided.

Discussion Questions

1. What is the appeal of the pro-choice position?
2. What kinds of strategies do pro-life supporters use?
3. Why would the pro-abortion or pro-choice positions be considered pro-women?
4. What is wrong with the statement "I'm personally not in favor of abortion, but I don't want to impose my view on others"?
5. Why are the pro-abortion and pro-choice positions really anti-women?
6. What kinds of choices do fetuses have?

Chapter Ten

The Problem of Unwanted Pregnancies

Our whole life would proceed in keeping with nature,
if we would but control our desires at the outset and refrain
from taking away with oils and vicious techniques the
human progeny born by the providence of God.
—Clement of Alexandria

In the simplest terms, a woman has an abortion because she does not desire to have the baby. This decision is precipitated for many reasons. The woman may be pregnant because she is the victim of an involuntary event, such as rape or incest. Preliminary medical reports may indicate that the fetus, if left to develop to term, may be born deformed or suffer from some serious medical disorder. It may be that the anticipated birth would bring severe economic hardship to the woman, and possibly to the rest of her family as well. Perhaps the expectant parents want a boy rather than a girl, or vice versa. Quite simply, the mother or both parents may not want to have children. Surely one of the most frequent situations is pregnancy out of wedlock. The social or familial embarrassment or trauma may loom so large that abortion offers a way of escape. These are only a few of the motivations for choosing abortion.

A common thread in all of these motivations is the perceived pain that a child's birth will bring. Abortion seems a quick and clean solution to that perceived pain, though a radical one.

Abortion and hedonism

Some people have characterized the culture in the United States as neo-hedonistic or the golden age of hedonism. Hedonism is often defined as a worldview or lifestyle marked by a vigorous pursuit of pleasure. More accurately, hedonism is an ethical philosophy in which the good is described as the maximum achievement of pleasure with the maximum avoidance of pain. It means grabbing all the gusto while having as few aches and pains as possible.

As a philosophy, hedonism has long had problems. Realizing that an unbridled pursuit of pleasure may bring as a consequence an abundance of undesired pain (for example, a pounding headache may follow overindulgence in the pleasures of alcohol), the ancient Epicureans sought to achieve a moderated and balanced quest for pleasure. There is a paradox in hedonism, because if we fail to achieve the pleasure we seek, we are frustrated, and if we gain the pleasure we seek, we tend to be bored. Thus, the pursuit of pleasure may be doomed to either frustration or boredom.

Hedonism as a formal ethic has few serious advocates beyond the likes of Hugh Hefner, but at the practical level we are all influenced by it. Unless we are masochists, most of us do not enjoy pain, so we eagerly seek ways to escape or at least diminish it. This is why the temptation to opt for abortion is so powerful. It is a way of escape.

Most pastors and physicians find it difficult to counsel a person to take a course of action that will be painful. This is perhaps the most demanding call of virtue. It is one thing to know what the good is; it is quite another to have the moral courage to pursue it while facing some kind of personal pain or loss. Yet self-sacrifice is at the heart of true virtue: Suffering pain in order to do what is right is the mark of a virtuous person. Doing what *feels* good is often easy. It's not so easy to do what *is* good. Cultural mores reach the bottom when an ethic like "If it feels good, do it" is embraced. Such slogans become the epitaphs of a corrupt society.

Not all concern for avoidance of future pain is selfish. Where there is a strong likelihood that the yet-to-be-born infant may face physical suffering due to disease or malformation, the concern may be directed toward the child.

Before further discussion of specific motives for abortion, it is important to make clear that the current national debate does not focus on therapeutic abortion or on abortion in the case of rape or incest. The great controversy concerns abortion on demand. Of course, therapeutic abortion and abortion in the case of rape or incest are important matters, but these particularly complex ethical issues should not cloud the central debate. Only a small number of abortions involve rape or incest, as we will see later in this chapter. Likewise, abortions performed to save the lives of women are exceedingly rare. The real issue is abortion for convenience or because the child is simply not wanted.

Justifying abortion on the grounds that the baby is unwanted is a perilous tack. If this motivation ignores the rights of the fetus, then the same reasoning could justify infanticide or other forms of homicide. I'm not suggesting that those who favor abortion when the baby is unwanted also advocate infanticide or homicide. The point is merely that if the undesirability of a living fetus is a just ethical ground for its destruction, the same principle would apply to other living humans. In other words, if it is unjust to kill a three-year-old child or a three-day-old child because he or she is undesired, then it is likewise unjust to kill a living human *before* birth. The bottom line is that undesirability is not a just moral basis to kill a human being.

Frequently, when a woman struggling with the question of abortion decides to continue her pregnancy, even though she does not want a baby, her thinking changes dramatically after her child's birth. When a mother sees and holds her offspring, a bonding often takes place that makes her wonder why she ever even considered abortion. Obviously, after an abortion it is too late for a woman to change her mind about the desirability of the child.

Some people justify abortion, even though the developing fetus may be alive or at least has potential life, since the child is destined to live in poverty or with some other social handicap. They say it is better to destroy the unborn baby before birth.

Certainly many people throughout history have despised the day they were born. Even biblical characters have cursed their births, Job and Jeremiah being the classic examples (Job 3:1–4, 11, 16; Jer. 20:18). Their lives involved such pain and torment that in crisis moments they wished they had never been born. Yet they went on to be people of great historical significance. As another example, anyone looking at the life prospects for Ludwig van Beethoven never would have guessed he had a chance to contribute much to human culture after he went blind.

Suicide is another indicator of extreme frustration with life. The number of suicides has risen in the United States, particularly among teenagers, among whom it is the second leading cause of death. Suicide, whatever its moral consequences, differs sharply from abortion in one critical respect—the suicide victim makes his or her own choice to live or die. As a living human being, I do not want someone else to decide whether the quality of my life is such that I should be destroyed.

The adoption option

As in any discussion of a highly charged issue, mistakes in logic are common in the abortion debate. One of these is the tendency for pro-abortion activists to commit "the false dilemma," often called the either/or fallacy of reasoning. In plain terms, this means that several options are incorrectly reduced to but two options. Of course, some questions clearly are limited to two options. For example, there either is a God (or gods) or there is not; either God exists or He does not—there is no middle alternative. However, just because some issues have only two options does not mean that all issues can validly be reduced to two options.

The either/or fallacy in the abortion question often joins with another false principle: the lesser of two evils. It goes like this: "Though abortion admittedly is not a pleasant option, it is preferable to the worse evil of having an unwanted child or a child whose quality of life may be undesirable." Therefore, abortion is justified as the lesser of two evils, and the fact that there are other alternatives is lost in the process.

The most obvious alternative to abortion is to put the baby up for adoption. In this way, the burden of having to care for an unwanted child after birth is removed from the pregnant woman. She still must face the considerable discomfort of pregnancy and the pain of childbirth. She may face parental disapproval, public shame, or scandal. Choosing the alternative of adoption may cost her a large price, but it is an honorable price. She will have acted justly and not compromised her integrity.

I chose the term *integrity* carefully. To have an abortion to avoid shame or scandal is not an act of integrity. Integrity is very much at the heart of this debate. To destroy a living fetus shows a lack of personal integrity.

Regrettably, the option of adoption currently is fraught with serious sociological problems. On the one hand, white couples face a desperate lack of adoptable white babies. Countless white couples, who earnestly desire to adopt, cannot find babies unless they are willing to adopt biracial or minority babies. Conversely, there are more minority and biracial babies being put up for adoption than there are families willing to adopt them. What is needed is not a decrease in the number of babies for adoption, but an increase in the demand. Pro-life activists need to model a willingness to adopt children of races different from their own.

Families who adopt children provide a model for pro-life activists. People who are deeply concerned about the abortion issue can accomplish something by going beyond protesting to the loving action of adopting unwanted children.

The problems of rape and incest

Abortions to end rape- and incest-caused pregnancies represent a very small number of cases and should be dealt with separately from the broader question of legalized abortion. As in all issues of human need and suffering, this requires absolute compassion. It is a small consolation to a rape victim who is pregnant to be told that she represents a tiny minority. Her problem is real.

In 2008, nearly ninety thousand forcible rapes were reported to authorities in the United States. Officials estimate, however, that the actual number of rapes is about four times as high as the number that is reported. If that is true, somewhere around three hundred and sixty thousand rapes occur in the United States every year.

Studies indicate that the rate of pregnancy from unprotected intercourse between fertile people is about three percent. If we apply that figure to the annual rape estimate, approximately ten thousand pregnancies occur each year from rape. However, the actual number is probably significantly lower.

Dr. Carolyn Gerstner offers reasons why the pregnancy rate in rapes is lower: (1) traumatic situations often immediately stifle ovulation; (2) the egg is fertile for only about twenty-four hours after ovulation; (3) the sperm remains viable for only forty-eight hours; (4) there may have been no actual penetration in the rape assault; (5) even if there was penetration, ejaculation may not have occurred; (6) rape victims range in age from infancy to one hundred years of age; only an unknown percentage fall into the fertility range of twelve to fifty years of age; (7) some victims of rape are infertile, sterile, or have had tubal ligation (many women use some form of birth control and are protected from pregnancy); and (8) the rapist may be sterile or have had a vasectomy. For these reasons, pregnancies from untreated rapes are rare.[52]

I want to point out that proper medical treatment administered immediately following a rape has a high degree of success in preventing pregnancy. *The Journal of the American Medical Association* of October 1971 documented 4,500 medically treated rape cases over a ten-year period in Minneapolis and Saint Paul, Minnesota. In these cases, there were no resulting pregnancies.

A more severe trauma is hard to imagine than that rare occasion when a woman becomes pregnant as a result of being raped. The victim had no choice in the matter of her pregnancy, and now she is left with a decision with respect to an undesired child. If the victim were my own daughter or a member of my church, I would counsel her to maintain the pregnancy on the grounds that the developing baby within her is a co-victim of the rapist's heinous crime. To kill the fetus, who is innocent of the offense, is to add insult to injury. I would want to move heaven and earth to secure an extraordinary support system for any woman put in this dreadful position and to seek compensation for her injury.

Therapeutic abortions

Abortions performed to save the life of a mother are almost non-existent, because advances in medical technology now largely prevent such situations. Yet it is possible that such an agonizing dilemma could happen. This brings the awful choice of deciding between the lesser of two evils. Do we destroy the baby to save the mother or risk the life of the mother to save the baby?

In principle, I opt for saving the baby, but I am not zealous to make that a matter of national law. This is an extremely vexing problem. If the choice is between allowing "nature" to kill the mother or "man" to kill the baby, I would choose the passive action of possibly letting a woman die from natural consequences rather than intervening to directly kill the unborn child. The excruciating issue is "passive" or "active" killing. Another reason to choose not to kill the child is the possibility that God will sustain the mother's life.

Other serious and difficult medical circumstances require complex ethical answers. It is beyond the scope of this book to address them. The central issue, however, must not be obscured or eclipsed by extreme cases of special difficulty. The national debate is not focused on such instances, nor should it be. The national issue is abortion on demand. Even if it were decided in extreme cases that abortion is an ethical option, the extreme cases should not dictate the general law.

Summary

- Some of the reasons given for abortion include anticipated economic hardship for the newborn child, the mother, or the family members; possible birth defects or other medical disorders; no desire to have children out of wedlock; and pregnancy as a result of rape or incest.
- Regardless of the reason for abortion, in all cases abortion is perceived as a "quick and clean" solution to anticipated pain.
- Only a small number of abortions are performed as a result of rape or incest. Therapeutic abortions—those done to save the life of the mother—are also rare.
- Adoption is one alternative to abortion. Because there is an oversupply of unwanted biracial and minority babies, pro-life adherents need to seriously consider adoption of such children.
- Extreme cases should not shift the focus of the abortion debate: The national issue is abortion on demand.

Discussion Questions

1. If abortion is homicide, can we ever allow it?
2. Is it wrong to seek pleasure and to avoid pain? Why or why not?
3. How can we show compassion and affirm the unborn baby's right to life in problem pregnancy situations?
4. Why are pro-abortion activists adamant in framing their argument around extremely rare pregnancy situations?
5. Who should decide whether a life with handicaps is worth living?
6. Are people with mental or physical disabilities fundamentally more unhappy than others?
7. Why is the Christian community reluctant to adopt "difficult to place" babies? What can be done to change this?

Part III

A COMPASSIONATE
RESPONSE AND STRATEGY

Chapter Eleven

Is Abortion the Unpardonable Sin?

*A woman on welfare who has six children and no husband
and who is desirous of an abortion does not have an immediate
need for a lecture on morals! . . . She of course needs to know
of the reconciling work of Christ, and when she responds to
His love, the Holy Spirit will quicken her to moral issues. . . .
Often by ministering to the physical, tangible need we
are privileged to meet the deeper spiritual one as well.*
—Bill Crouse

The Christian church is the only army that shoots its wounded.
—Unknown

Since the Bible mentions an unforgivable sin, there has been
much speculation concerning its specific identity. Some people
have jumped to the conclusion that abortion is the unforgivable sin, because murder is one of the most heinous of sins and

abortion has been considered a form of murder. Is this a valid conclusion concerning the unforgivable sin? No.

Without delving into the theological technicalities, let me say categorically that there is no biblical evidence to support the idea and considerable evidence to deny that abortion is the unforgivable sin.

King David was guilty of murder; for his personal gain, he conspired to have Uriah killed. David wanted to marry Uriah's wife, Bathsheba. David's remorse over his sin is a model of biblical contrition. His prayer of repentance in Psalm 51 is classic. We have every reason to believe that, even after his compound sins of adultery and murder, David was forgiven and restored to fellowship with God. There is no less reason to believe that those who undergo abortions may be forgiven, too.

How God deals with sin and guilt

Personal guilt may be the reason some people are concerned about the possibility that abortion is unforgivable. People who are devoutly religious and who endeavor to follow the ethics of the Bible struggle with the same sins that everybody else does. It would be foolish to assume that abortion occurs only outside the membership of the church. I do not know about specific behavior in all church groups, but I do know that within the circle of so-called evangelical churches, abortion is more than an isolated reality. It may even be at epidemic levels. Since evangelical Christians have often been at the forefront of the pro-life movement, we see an immediate moral contradiction. With the contradiction come severe moral conflict and much unresolved guilt.

I vividly recall a sad episode that occurred when I was called to the bedside of a Christian woman dying of uterine cancer. She was in the final stages of her illness and had requested the sacrament of the Lord's Supper. I went to the hospital to comfort her and to administer the sacrament. During our meeting, she expressed great emotional distress and concern about her soul. She told me she had carried a secret guilt for a long time, something she had not told even her husband—she had had an abortion. She asked me whether I thought her cancer was a punishment sent from God because of her sin.

In such a situation, a pastor often gives the patient unqualified assurance that God would never do such a thing as inflict cancer on a person as punishment for sin. Such consolations, however, are not grounded in truth. The Bible reveals that God may and sometimes does administer temporal punishment for temporal guilt in the form of disease or even death. God afflicted Miriam and King Uzziah with a disease for their sins. Both were stricken by leprosy as acts of divine judgment (Num. 12:1, 9–11; 2 Chron. 26:16, 19–21).

On the other hand, the Bible also warns against assuming that an affliction is a sign of divine discipline. The entire book of Job dispels that notion, as well as Jesus' teaching in John 9 regarding the man who was born blind. (I have written a book on this perplexing subject titled *Surprised by Suffering*.) It is wrong to conclude that suffering is always an indication of divine punishment. We are equally wrong to assert that it is never an indication of divine punishment. All that can be said for sure is that it *may* be an indication of divine punishment.

I explained to the dying woman that I did not know the secret counsel of God and could not say what His purpose was for her affliction. I could tell her with certainty, however, that God forgives anyone who repents. I mentioned the comforting promise of 1 John 1:9: "If we confess our sins, he is faithful and just to forgive us our sins and cleanse us from all unrighteousness." Here God promises to forgive and cleanse our sins if we confess them to Him in a repentant spirit.

This verse echoes similar promises in the Bible:

"Come now, let us reason together, says the LORD:
though your sins are like scarlet, they shall be as white as
    snow;
though they are red like crimson, they shall become like
    wool." (Isa. 1:18)

Create in me a clean heart, O God, and renew a right
    spirit within me.
Cast me not away from your presence, and take not your
    Holy Spirit from me.
Restore to me the joy of your salvation, and uphold me
    with a willing spirit.
Then I will teach transgressors your ways, and sinners
    will return to you.
Deliver me from bloodguiltiness, O God,
O God of my salvation,

and my tongue will sing aloud of your righteousness.
O Lord, open my lips,
and my mouth will declare your praise.
For you will not delight in sacrifice, or I would give it;
you will not be pleased with a burnt offering.
The sacrifices of God are a broken spirit;
a broken and contrite heart, O God, you will not
    despise. (Ps. 51:10–17)

In the passage from Isaiah, God promises to change the sins of His people from the stain of scarlet and crimson to the whiteness of snow or wool. This brings to mind the torments of guilt that plagued Lady Macbeth. She could not find soap strong enough to remove the stain of guilt from her bloody hands. Yet God's forgiving grace is able to remove that stain completely.

David understood that guilt is not removed by offering sacrifices or by trying to make up for it by good works, but that God requires a broken and contrite heart. God does not grant forgiveness without a condition. We often hear that God gives unconditional acceptance and forgiveness. Such an idea is totally foreign to the biblical teaching on forgiveness. God demands that a condition be met. He requires earnest repentance and confession as the terms by which He will fully and freely forgive.

Thousands of people struggle with guilt connected with abortion. It haunts women who have had them, men who have encouraged them, and doctors who have performed them. One doctor reported in *The New York Times* that she had to prepare herself emotionally and often endured sleepless nights before performing abortions: "It's a very tough thing for a gynecologist to do," she said. "The emotions it arouses are so strong . . . that doctors don't talk to each other about it." On one occasion, this doctor collapsed on the floor, overcome by emotion, after performing an abortion.[53]

Guilt is a powerful emotion, one that has the capacity to inflict severe psychological paralysis on people. I once was approached by a practicing psychiatrist with an offer to join his staff. He explained that a large number of his patients were suffering from problems related to severe guilt. "These people don't need a doctor, they need a priest," he said. "They need someone to tell them they are forgiven."

This psychiatrist had no loyalty to Christianity; he was simply concerned about the mental health of his patients. He understood the devastating power of unresolved guilt, and he recognized that denial and rationalization were not effective means of dealing with real guilt. The only effective cure for real guilt is real forgiveness. To try to cover the stain on our hands is a poor substitute for having the stain removed.

Experiencing God's forgiveness

To experience the profound liberation of forgiveness, one must simply go to God and confess the sin with a humble heart and a contrite spirit. Contrition involves a genuine and godly sorrow for having disobeyed God. It differs from the repentance of attrition, which is a false form of repentance motivated by a fear of punishment. Attrition is seen in a child who, when he sees a paddle in his mother's hand, is sorry that he got caught with his hand in the cookie jar. True repentance acknowledges the reality of the guilt and does not try to justify it. Anyone who approaches God with true humility, contrition, and an earnest resolution not to commit the sin again will surely receive the forgiveness of God.

We often hear the question, "If you had the opportunity to live your life over again, what would you do differently?" Sometimes people answer by saying they would do everything exactly the same. I have a hard time believing that. All of us have things in our past for which we are ashamed. In my case, there are things I have said that I wish I hadn't spoken. But once a word escapes from my lips, I cannot call it back. It is like an arrow released from a bow. I can change my words or apologize for my words, but once they are uttered they cannot be recalled. What has been done cannot be undone. It is a matter of history.

Though what I have done cannot be undone, I can be forgiven. Forgiveness is one of the marvels of God's grace. Its healing power is magnificent. If a woman has been involved in abortion, God does not require that she spend the rest of her life walking around with a red "A" on her chest. He does require that she repent of her sin and come to Him for the cleansing of forgiveness. When God forgives us, we are forgiven. When God cleanses us, we are made clean. That is a cause for great celebration.

Summary

- There is no biblical evidence to support the idea that abortion is the unpardonable sin.

- God forgives anyone who humbly and contritely repents of sin—even the sin of abortion.

Discussion Questions

1. How do non-Christians deal with guilt?
2. If God will forgive, why shouldn't a Christian have an abortion?
3. How do Christians usually respond to women who seek or have had an abortion?
4. What are the psychological effects of having an abortion? Of performing one?
5. What role in the abortion issue can the Christian church uniquely fulfill?
6. How can we know that we are forgiven?

Chapter Twelve

A Pro-Life Strategy

Not only for every idle word but for
every idle silence must man render an account.
—Ambrose of Milan

All that is necessary for evil to triumph
is for good men to do nothing.
—Edmund Burke

Those who are alarmed by legalized abortion and who are devoted to the pro-life position frequently ask, "What can I do?" Dedicated people and groups have been working on this issue ever since the Supreme Court legalized abortion. Considerable public interest in the issue has been aroused, but abortion remains legal. There is much to be done if the situation is ever to be rectified.

Those struggling for the unborn's fundamental right to live should be encouraged by William Wilberforce's struggle to abolish slavery in the British empire. Year after frustrating year, his efforts were defeated by Parliament. He was harassed, maligned, ridiculed, and slandered. Wilberforce was sharply criticized for raising religious objections against the slave trade. On one occasion, Lord Melbourne stated, "Things have come to a pretty pass when religion is allowed to invade public life."[54] Doesn't that sound like today's media quotes in the United States?

Wilberforce, in the heat of his struggle against slavery, received the following encouraging letter from John Wesley:

> My dear sir,
>
> Unless the Divine power has raised you up as Athanasius *contra mundum*, I do not see how you can go through your glorious enterprise in opposing that execrable villainy, which is the scandal of religion, of England, and of human nature. Unless God has raised you up for this very thing, you will be worn out by the opposition of men and devils, but if God is for you who can be against you? Are all of them together stronger than God? Oh, be not weary of well-doing. Go in the name of God, and in the power of His might, till even American slavery, the vilest that ever saw the sun, shall vanish away before it. That He that has guided you from your youth up may continue to strengthen in this and all things, is the prayer of
>
> Your affectionate servant,
> John Wesley[55]

Wilberforce died on July 29, 1833—three days after the Bill For the Abolition of Slavery passed its second reading in the

House of Commons, sounding the end for slavery. "Thank God," he whispered on his deathbed, "that I should have lived to witness a day in which England was willing to give twenty million sterling for the abolition of slavery."[56]

Wilberforce's example of steadfastness across more than three decades illustrates not only a heroic victory against an unspeakable crime, but also the cost of such a mission. The pain Wilberforce endured in his struggle against slavery was immeasurable.

Resistance to unjust laws and dehumanizing practices may be costly. Those who resisted Adolf Hitler's policy of genocide in Germany often paid with their lives. Dietrich Bonhoeffer, the pastor who wrote *The Cost of Discipleship*, was one who paid such a price. The world still recoils in horror at the reality of the Holocaust in Nazi Germany. Yet I believe we are in the midst of a new and more evil holocaust, which sees the destruction of 1.5 million unborn babies every year in the United States alone. This situation calls to mind the words of a German pastor imprisoned for opposing Hitler. Martin Niemoller said:

> In Germany they came first for the Communists, and I didn't speak up because I wasn't a Communist. They came for the Jews, and I didn't speak up because I wasn't a Jew. Then they came for the trade unionists, and I didn't speak up because I wasn't a trade unionist. Then they came for the Catholics, and I didn't speak up because I was a Protestant. Then they came for me, and by that time no one was left to speak up.[57]

If you care about the slaughter of the innocent, then for God's sake, speak up. Speak to your family. Speak to your neighbor. Speak to your friend. Speak to your doctor. Speak to your minister. Speak to your congressman. Let your voice be heard in a chorus of protest. Yours is only one voice, but it is a voice. Use it.

Strategic target: pro-choice adherents

In the past, the number one target of anti-abortion activists has been the abortion clinic. The advantage of this strategy is that it presses the issue and focuses public attention on the point where the offense occurs. The disadvantage of this target is that it involves people who are firmly convinced of their pro-abortion position.

As we have already seen, the pivotal group in shaping cultural opinion is the middle-ground, pro-choice group. Here is the most fertile field for finding people who will cross over to the pro-life position. It is always a good strategy to concentrate efforts on the most likely prospects.

Strategic target: liberal churches and liberals

Though much public protest has taken place around abortion clinics, little or no public protest has occurred around churches where the pastors have adopted the pro-choice position. Sadly, the organized church—more than any other institution apart from the Supreme Court—has neglected its duty to inform the public conscience.

One reason pro-choice churches have not been targeted is because of the perceived cleavage between conservative and liberal Christians. The split on the abortion issue between conservative and liberal churches is a strange phenomenon. In the past, the two groups have tended to divide over personal-redemption agendas versus social-action agendas. In the case of the abortion dispute, conservative churchmen have been at the forefront of the pro-life movement while the liberal churches have tended to be pro-choice.

As I discussed in chapter 9, this division is due largely to the pro-abortion activists' successful linkage of the abortion issue with feminism. Liberal churches have so vigorously supported the women's-liberation movement that they have accepted the pro-choice position as part of the package. This has created an almost bizarre liberal contradiction.

Historically, liberals have been at the forefront of human-rights issues. Traditionally, they have opposed slavery and racial discrimination, and they have been zealous in the cause of human dignity. However, when the crucial issue of the dignity of life pertains to the unborn, the liberal community is strangely absent or on the wrong side of the issue, largely because of the perceived strategic link abortion has with feminist issues. In their zeal to protect women's rights, liberals have sacrificed the rights of the unborn.

The multitudes of honest liberals who have strong convictions about human dignity and foundational human rights would seem to be ripe for reversal of their position on abortion. These people need to be encouraged to look more deeply into the underlying human life issue that is central to the abortion debate.

Strategic target: the medical community

Unlike ancient Greece, where the physicians led the public out-cry against abortion, the medical community in the United States often has been either tacitly supportive of abortion or strangely quiet. The medical community has the greatest financial vested interest in abortion, which has become at least a billion-dollar business. Abortion has brought a shadow of doubt across the landscape of the medical profession. Doctors once enjoyed a high degree of respect as the heroic protectors of human life. Now in some quarters many doctors are viewed as crass money grubbers who destroy human life in exchange for money.

Doctors who regularly perform abortions are receiving some backlash from their colleagues. *The New York Times* reported the following:

> Under siege from protestors and largely isolated from medical colleagues, doctors who perform abortions say they are being heavily stigmatized, and fewer and fewer doctors are willing to enter the field. Reflecting the public's ambivalence about abortion, many doctors on both sides of the issue say they find abortions emotionally difficult and unpleasant.

> A 1985 poll by the American College of Obstetricians and Gynecologists of 4000 of its 29000 members reported that 84% said they thought abortions should be legal and available, but only a third of the doctors who

favored abortions actually performed them and two-thirds of those who did abortions did very few.

About four percent of those polled performed 26 or more abortions a month. The researchers did not ask the doctors why they did or did not perform abortions. "The term *abortionist* still has a very heavy stigma," said Dr. Curtis E. Harris, an obstetrician in Oklahoma City who heads the American Academy of Medical Ethics, a group of 21,000 doctors that favors greatly restricting availability of abortions.

"Most gynecologists work to bring a child into the world in a healthy state," Dr. Harris said, adding that performing an abortion "is a real contradiction."

With few incentives to perform abortions, most obstetricians and gynecologists avoid them, medical experts say and surveys of doctors report. Those who support abortion rights say the shortage of willing doctors makes it harder for women, who sometimes have to travel hundreds of miles to find a doctor to abort a fetus. . . .

Dr. Warren Hern, who directs the Boulder Abortion Clinic in Colorado, said, "Abortion doctors are treated as a pariah by the medical community," adding, "At best, we are tolerated."[58]

For those of us who are vigorously opposed to abortion, this report is good news. A serious ethical and professional struggle is going on within the medical community. At this level, pro-life strategists need to turn up the heat. Every pro-life activist should make it a point to ask his or her physician whether he or she does abortions or refers patients to abortionists. If the answer to either question is yes, a boycott is in order.

A boycott could be justified not only on strategic anti-abortion grounds, but also on the grounds of common sense in the area of medical care. Though the Third Reich's Joseph Mengele may have been a brilliant experimental physician, I would not have wanted to place the life of my wife in his hands. Though doctors who perform abortions may have a high degree of technical medical skill, their practice betrays their less-than-adequate respect for the sanctity of life. Personally, I wouldn't risk my body or the bodies of my family to anyone who exhibits such a low view of life.

Strategic target: politicians and public officials

Pro-life activists need to pressure politicians who are so directly responsible for legislation. Candidates for office need to hear from us. There have been bold and courageous elected officials who have suffered for the cause of the rights of the unborn. They need our encouragement and support. Likewise, the president of the United States needs encouragement for his leadership in this struggle.

Dr. C. Everett Koop, the former surgeon general of the United States, was positively heroic in his outspoken opposition to abortion. Presidential administrations have come and gone, but quite frankly, the pro-abortion presidents have had far more effect on the issue than the pro-life presidents.

Strategic target: parents and the family

Since a high percentage of abortions are sought by teenage unwed mothers, the role of parents in the decision-making process is important. In many cases, parents are not involved because they have no knowledge of the situation. One motivation for abortion among young women is to conceal their pregnancies from their parents out of fear of punishment.

In other cases, parents urge young women to choose abortion. The motivations for such counsel vary. Sometimes the goal is to ease the burden of an unwanted pregnancy. Other times, however, the parents' counsel is motivated by a desire to escape or avoid scandal or embarrassment in the parents' own social sphere.

As a pastor, I have encountered parental pressure for abortion in homes where the parents profess to be Christians. This indicates a need for Christian parents to be educated in the ethics of abortion and to teach the biblical ethic to their children. God does more than encourage such instruction—He commands it (see Deut. 6).

The strategy of civil disobedience

Attempts at abortion clinics to rescue the unborn from destruction have received widespread media coverage. The strategy involves the intentional violation of trespassing laws in order to peaceably block the entrances to abortion clinics. Thousands of Americans have been arrested for participating in these rescue events, including my own son, who cooled his heels in a

Mississippi jail. This practice—which involves intentional civil disobedience—is hotly disputed even within the ranks of pro-life activists.

Is this activity a legitimate form of civil disobedience? Some pro-life activists seek to justify it on the grounds of a "necessary defense" plea. They argue that if a person runs into a burning building to save someone who is trapped inside, under the law he cannot be convicted for trespass violations. The problem with this argument is that when someone is rescued from a fire, the law recognizes the trapped person as a living human being. Unfortunately, when a baby is rescued from death by abortion, the law does not recognize the unborn person as a living human being.

The Bible has a high view of the sanctity of life and of civil obedience. This is the issue that divides Christians. It's the same issue that Bonhoeffer had to struggle with when he was invited to join a plot to assassinate Hitler. We must draw the line between what is a legitimate form of protest and what is not. It is no easy question to solve, and I must confess that I have not resolved it in my own mind. However, the urgency of the abortion issue requires us to protest to the very limit that our consciences allow.

The struggle must continue

The struggle against abortion is difficult, but it is worthy. The longer it lasts, the more babies will be slain. The longer laws allowing abortion on demand remain in effect, the more likely it is that society will become hardened in heart. Continuing the struggle against abortion is not enough. We must accelerate our efforts until no human child is destroyed under the sanction of law.

Summary

- The struggle against abortion is difficult and may require significant personal sacrifice.
- The middle-ground, pro-choice advocate may be the best strategic target for the pro-life movement.
- Other targets for pro-life activity include liberal churches, liberals who support human-rights issues, physicians and other medical personnel, politicians and public officials, and Christian parents and their children.
- The degree to which any person will go to protest abortion is a matter of personal conscience. However, everyone who is pro-life can at least speak out and make pro-life opinions known.

Discussion Questions

1. What strategies have been most effective for the pro-life movement? What strategies have been least effective?
2. What are our responsibilities to pregnant women who opt against abortion?
3. Should pro-life activists hold protests at churches that are pro-choice? What kind of impact would this have?

4. What place does emotion properly have in regard to the abortion issue?

5. What kinds of pressure can be put on the medical community?

6. What can Christian parents do to educate their children regarding abortion?

7. Why are we reluctant to be active in this cause? What would inspire greater activity?

Appendix A

Testimony on the
Beginning of Human Life

As medical technology advances and becomes more complex, our ethical questions tend to become more complex as well. One breakthrough, in-vitro fertilization, which allows previously barren women to have children, has been a particularly difficult ethical issue. More than two decades ago, a Tennessee court heard a case in which a divorcing couple argued over rights to their frozen embryos. While this case does not deal directly with the issue of abortion, it does address a foundational issue: some of the scientific discoveries on the beginning of human life.

The following transcript is a portion of the court proceedings (Circuit Court Blount County, state of Tennessee, Maryville, August 10, 1989) in which Jerome Lejeune, M.D., Ph.D., testified. (Some testimony that was not relevant to the main issue was deleted.) Dr. Lejeune (1926–94) was professor of fundamental genetics on the faculty of Medicine of Paris, held the Kennedy Prize (for being first to discover a disease caused by chromosomal

155

abnormality—Down's syndrome), and was a member of a number of prestigious medical and scientific organizations.

Dr. Lejeune's native language was French. His testimony was recorded as he spoke in English, a foreign language to him.

Mr. Christenberry, Mr. Clifford, and Mr. Taylor were the lawyers. "The Court" indicates statements made by the judge. "The Witness" indicates testimony given by Dr. Lejeune.

MR. CHRISTENBERRY: I believe at this time, your Honor, I would ask the Court to recognize Dr. Lejeune as an expert witness in the field in which he's here to testify.

THE COURT: Any objection?

MR. CLIFFORD: Your Honor, we certainly recognize Dr. Lejeune's expertise in the field of genetics.

MR. CHRISTENBERRY: Thank you, your Honor.

Q. Thank you. With respect to the issues in this case, you understand the—what we would say is the factual understanding of how Mr. Davis feels and how Mrs. Davis feels. There has been some publicity about this, has there not, Doctor? You have heard something about their dilemma?

A. I heard something, but very little. I must be very honest, I don't look at television, I don't listen to the radio, and I only knew when Mr. Palmer telephoned to me, that was the first time I heard about it. So I would not say I'm really knowing the whereabouts, no. I know there are babies, there are human beings in the fridge, this is the only thing I know.

Q. Thank you, Doctor. So let's start with that aspect of this case. You're familiar with in-vitro fertilization?

A. Yes.

Q. When did you write your first article about it, if you recall?

A. Oh, you are terrible with dates; I'm not good with the answers. It must be fifteen years ago, something.

Q. Okay.

A. Before it was used.

Q. Before it was used. So before it was used it had been conceived in man's mind, had it not?

A. Well, you have to understand that artificial fertilization is something rather old in biology, and it was used for animals long before it was applied to man. And what seems today extraordinary, that is freezing a human embryo, it was not extraordinary for a cow. There is a lot of time that cows have been frozen and used and sent by air mail in little containers. And the novelty is to consider that the technique, which was devised for husbandry, was good enough for mankind.

Q. Tell us about in-vitro fertilization and your view of it and your perspective that you could offer today.

A. Well, could I speak more about nature—

Q. Yes.

A. —of the human being, than specifically the condition in-vitro, because to understand what means the fertilization in-vitro, we have to understand what means fertilization at the beginning of a human being.

Q. All right.

A. And if I can say so, I would say that life has a very long history, but each of us has a unique beginning, the moment of conception. We know and all the genetics and all the zoology are there to tell us that there is a link between the parents and the children. And this link is made of a long molecule that we can dissect, the DNA molecule, which is transmitting information from parents to children through generations and generations. As soon as the program is written on the DNA, there are twenty-three different pieces of program carried by the spermatazoa and there are twenty-three different homologous pieces carried by the ovum. As soon as the twenty-three chromosomes carried by the sperm encounter the twenty-three chromosomes carried by the ovum, the whole information necessary and sufficient to spell out all the characteristics of the new being is gathered.

Q. Is what, sir?

A. Gathered.

Q. Gathered.

A. Gathered. And it's very interesting, if I can say, your Honor, to remark that natural sciences and science of the law, in fact, speak the same language. In that sense that when we see somebody healthy, well built, we say he has a robust constitution, and when we see a country in which every subject is protected by the law, we say it has an equitable constitution. In the phenomenon of the writing a law, you have to spell out every term of the law before it can be considered to be a law. I mean in the science of the law. And secondarily, this information written in the law has to be enacted, and it cannot be before it has been voted for.

Now, life does exactly the same thing. Inside the chromosomes is written the program and all the definitions. In fact, chromosomes are, so to speak, the table of the law of life. If you get the right number of your table of the law of your life, then you begin your own life. Now, the voting process does exist as well. It is the fertilization itself, because there are a lot of proposals, many, many sperms. Only one got in; that is the voting process, which enacts the new constitution of a man. And exactly as would say a lawyer, once a constitution exists in a country, you can speak about it in the same way, when this information carried by the sperm and by the ovum has encountered each other, then a new human being is defined because its own personal and human constitution is entirely spelled out.

There exists a lot of minute differences in the message given by father and the one given by mother, even by the same person; we do not give exactly the same minute information in each sperm or in each egg. It follows that the voting process of the fertilization produces a personal constitution which is entirely typical of this very one human being which has never occurred before and will never occur again. It's an entire novelty. That was sure—that was known for let's say not a hundred years but more than fifty years. But the bewildering was the minuteness of the writing of those tables of the law.

You have to figure out what is a DNA molecule. I would say it's a long thread of one meter (sic) of length, cut in twenty-three pieces. Each piece is coiled on itself very tightly to make spiral of spiral of spiral so that finally it looks like a little rod that we can see under the microscope that we call a chromosome. And there are twenty-three of them carried by father, twenty-three of them carried by mother. I said the minuteness of the language is bewildering because if I was bringing here in the Court all the one-meter-long DNA of the sperms and all the meter-long of the ovums which will make every one of the five billions of human beings that will replace ourselves in this planet, this amount of matter would be roughly two aspirin tablets. That tells us that nature to carry the information from father to children, from mother to children, from generation to generation has used the smallest possible language. And it is very necessary because life is taking advantage of the movement of the particles, of molecules, to put order inside the chance development of random movement of particles, so that chance is now transformed according to the necessity of the new being.

All the information being written they have to be written in the smallest language possible so that they can dictate how to manipulate particle by particle, atom by atom, molecule by molecule. We have to be with life at the real cross between matter, energy, and information.

Now, I would like, your Honor, to give you an impression of what happens normally. Most of the human beings have been conceived before the fertilization in-vitro was used, and most of the humanity will still be made the old good days' fashion for a long time I do hope. Normally, when the ovum is ripe, that is, once a month, fifteen days after the menses, there is a rupture of the follicle, and the ovum is so to speak taken by the fallopian tube, which has a special expansion—we call it *le pavilion*—I don't know the name in English. And it can move, and if you take a picture it looks like as a hand making a slow palpation of the ovary to find where the egg will be laid and to take it.

Normally, the egg is a big cell, round, not mobile, floating quietly inside the fluid in the tube, and the tube will manage to carry this big cell towards the uterus by ciliate movements. On the contrary, the sperm is an indefatigable navigator. It has been deposited in the entry of the genitalia of the mother, and normally it goes up through the cervix of the uterus, he swims during the whole uterine cavity, and it is inside the fallopian tube that the encounter between few thousands, ten thousands, hundred thousands of sperm and the one egg can occur. And it is because every human being has been conceived in nature inside the little tube, a tube of flesh that we call the fallopian tube, that test tube babies are indeed possible. The only difference is that sperm and egg are meeting inside a tube which is now a tube of glass because the egg has been removed from the body of the woman, and the sperm has been just added to the little vessel. And it's because normal *fecundation*—I should say fertilization in English—normal fertilization is occurring inside a tube that if you put the proper medium . . . It is not at all the inseminator who makes fertilization, he just puts on the right medium, a ripe ovum, active sperm, and it is the sperm who made the fertilization. Man would be unable to make a fertilization. It has to be done directly by the cells. And it's because they were normally floating in the fluid that this extracorporeal technique is at all possible.

Now, the reproduction process is a very impressive phenomenon in the sense that what is reproduced is never the matter, but it is information. For example, when you want to reproduce a statue, you can make a mold and there will be an exact contiguity between the atoms of the original statue and the atoms of the mold. During the molding process there will be again between the plaster and the mold contact atom by atom so that you reproduce the statue. But what is reproduced is not the original because you can make it out of plaster, out of bronze, about anything. What is reproduced is the form that the genius of the sculptor had imprinted in the matter. The same thing is true for any reproduction, whether it is by radio, by television, by photography, what is printed or reproduced is the information and not the matter. The matter is a support of the information. And that explains to us how life is at all possible, because it would be impossible to reproduce matter. Matter is not living, matter cannot live at all. Matter is matter. What is reproduced and transmitted, it's an information which will animate matter. Then there is nothing like living matter, what exists is animated matter. And what we learn in genetics is to know what does animate the matter, to force the matter to take the form of a human being.

To give you an idea, I would take a very simple example, I would take the example of this little apparatus here, a recorder.

Q. Yes, sir.

A. Now, chromosomes are a long thread of DNA in which information is written. They are coiled very tightly on the chromosomes, and, in fact, a chromosome is very comparable to a mini-cassette, in which a symphony is written, the symphony of life. Now, exactly as if you go and buy a cartridge on which the *Kleine Nachtmusik* from Mozart has been registered, if you put it in a normal recorder, the musician would not be reproduced, the notes of music will not be reproduced, they are not there; what would be reproduced is the movement of air which transmits to you the genius of Mozart. It's exactly the same way that life is played. On the tiny mini-cassettes which are our chromosomes are written various parts of the opus which is for human symphony, and as soon as all the information necessary and sufficient to spell out the whole symphony, this symphony plays itself, that is, a new man is beginning his career.

In-vitro fertilization does not change at all what I have said. It's just a technique sometime used to bypass a difficulty in the encounter of the egg and the sperm, so it's a—it's a derivation. It does not change at all the basic mechanism, the basic mechanism is just the same.

Now, if I could continue a little more, it's not about fertilization that we are discussing. It's about freezing of embryos. I'm not a specialist at freezing embryos. Your Honor, I have never played with embryos. But in my laboratory we are freezing cells, we are thawing them, we are using a lot of those processes, so we know about it, we use it on another system than embryos, but all cells are very similar in their reactions. Now, you have to realize—I don't know if it is true in English, but I think it's quite true, and it is true at least in all the Latin language, we use the same word to define the tempo that we measure with a clock and the temperature that we measure with a thermometer. We say in French *temps* and *temperature*; in English you say *time* which is a change of tempo, which is a temporal thing, and *temperature*. And that is not a mistake of the ordinary language; it's a definition of the basic phenomenon. I don't know how they have recognized it so long ago to build it into the language. What means "time" is the flux of the agitation of the molecule, the flux of the particle which is continually going on. And temperature is just a measure of the speed with which the molecules are running in a given medium.

Now, if you diminish progressively temperature, you diminish the speed and the number of collisions between the molecules, and so to speak without any joke about the words, you are progressively slowing down, slowing down the temperature, you are freezing time. And, in fact, we are wrong telling that we are freezing embryos. In a sense it's very true like you deep freeze the meat in the supermarket, very correct. But in the fundamental sense what we are doing by lowering down the temperature is stopping not totally but very deeply the movements of the atoms and molecule so, in fact, inside the can, the thermal can in which we put in tiny canisters the cells or the embryos, we have more or less arrested the flux of the time. This seems to be rhetorical, but it is not because otherwise we could never understood why it is possible to freeze a cell, to have it entirely not moving, not respiring, not having any chemical exchange, and just if you have done it with precision (so that no crystals have been made inside the cells which could have ruptured its very minute architecture), if you thaw it, thaw it progressively and carefully, it will again begin to flourish and to divide. Then it's obviously sure that we have not arrested life and started life again. What we have arrested is the time for this particular organism which is inside this can.

If we could put a cell down to the minus two hundred seventy-three centigrade, that is, to the absolute zero, every movement would be stopped. And if the temperature would be maintained at that level, it would be kept unchanged for indefinity. I would not say eternity but indefinity. We are not achieving that when we freeze a cell in my laboratory (and you do the same here); we use not liquid hydrogen because it's very costly and very explosive, and it's used only in NASA for the rockets. We use mostly liquid nitrogen because it cannot explode, and it's rather cheap, and it's easy to manage. But it's only minus a hundred ninety degrees that we have inside the canister. Well, it's rather cool, but it's not absolute zero, so the preservation is not a hundred percent.

And probably you could not preserve the cells for more than a number of years; that nobody knows because it depends on the cells. For example, to the best of my knowledge for ordinary cells which are very resistant, they are examples of more than fifteen years in the canister and being thawed and being correctly surviving and alive. For mouse embryo it's some ten years. In our species I think there are no long time, maybe one or two years, no more than that. And nobody knows with the actual technique how long the preservation would be real preservation. It's a question I could not answer, and I think nobody can answer precisely today.

But what I could say, that the information which is inside this first cell obviously tell to this cell all the tricks of the trade to build herself as the individual, this cell is already. I mean it's not a definition to build a theoretical man, but to build that particular human person we will call later Margaret or Paul or Peter; it's already there, but it's so small that we cannot see it. It's by induction that we know it for the moment. And I would say I would like to use the felicitous expression of the mathematicians. They would say that man is reduced at its simplest expression like you can do with an algebraic formula if you manipulate it intelligently. If you want to know what mean that formula you have to expand it to give value to the various parameters, and to put in use a formula, you expand it. It's what is life, the formula is there; if you allow this formula to be expanded by itself, just giving shelter and nurture, then you have the development of the full person.

Now, I know that there has been recent discussion of vocabulary, and I was very surprised two years ago that some of our British colleagues invented the term of pre-embryo. That does not exist, it has never existed. I was curious, and I went to the encyclopedia, to the French encyclopedia, the one I inherited from my great father, so it was fifty years ago it was printed. And at the term of *embryo* it was said: "The youngest form of a being," which is very clear and simple definition, and it stated: "It starts as one fertilized cell, (fertilized egg which is called also *zygote*), and when the zygote splits in two cells, it is called a two-cell embryo. When it split in four it is called a four-cell embryo." Then it's very interesting because this terminology was accepted the world over for more than fifty years by all the specialists of the world, and we had no need at all of a sub-class which would be called a pre-embryo, because there is nothing before the embryo. Before an embryo there is a sperm and an egg, and that is it. And the sperm and an egg cannot be a pre-embryo because you cannot tell what embryo it will be, because you don't know what the sperm will go in what an egg, but once it is made, you have got a zygote and when it divides it's an embryo and that's it.

I think it's important because people would believe that a pre-embryo does not have the same significance that an embryo. And in fact, on the contrary, a first cell knows more and is more specialized, if I could say, than any cell which is later in our organism.

Now, I don't know if I can abuse of your patience, your Honor?

THE COURT: You're doing fine.

THE WITNESS: The very young human being, just after fertilization, after it has split in two cells and then in three cells because curiously we do not split ourselves in two, four, eight and continue like that, no, at the beginning we don't do that. We split in two cells of roughly equal dimension and one of the two cells splits in two. There is a moment in which inside the *zona pellucida* which is a kind of plastic bag, which is, so to speak, the wall of the private life of the embryo in which it is protected from the outside, we have a stage in which there are three cells. This has been known for fifty, sixty years, and it was remaining a mystery for embryology, because after that stage of three cells, it starts again, it comes to four, and it continue by multiples of two.

What could be the meaning? We do not know yet the accurate meaning, but it is of great importance about the discussion we have today because we can manipulate non-human embryos like, for example, mice. We can disassemble the cells which are inside the *zona pellucida* of a sixteen-cell embryo of mice and take few cells of it, take few cells from another embryo, of another type of embryo, if you wish, and put all that together inside a new *zona pellucida* from which you have expelled the legitimate occupant.

Now, what happens? Most of the time it fails, but sometimes a chimera comes out. For example, if you have chosen a black embryo, a white embryo and you have mixed them together, you find a little tiny mouse which can run on your table but which has a chessboard on the body. Parts are black, parts are white because she has built herself of two type of cells that you had put together in the same *zona pellucida*. It has to be done with a very small number of cells.

We have tried, and when I say we, I should say geneticists, have tried to put three different lines, and they have got few mice with three different type of cells that they can see on the fur. They have tried four, does not work; five, does not work. It's only possible with three cells. And that remembers that when we split at the beginning of our life (two cells and then one cell in two), we go at a three-cell stage. It's probably at that time that a message goes from one cell to the two other cells, come back to the first one and suddenly realize we are not a population of cells. We are bound to be an individual. This is individualization, that makes the difference between a population of cells which is just a tissue culture and an individual which will build himself according to his own rule, is demonstrated at the three-cell stage, that is very soon after fertilization has occurred.

If we stop the process, if we slow down the movement of the molecules, we progressively come to a relative standstill, and when the embryo is frozen, these tiny human beings, they are very small, one millimeter and a half of a dimension, a sphere a millimeter and a half, you can put them in canisters by the thousands. And then with the due connotation, the fact of putting inside a very chilly space, tiny human beings who are deprived of liberty, of any movement, even they are deprived of time (time is frozen for them), make them surviving, so to speak, in a suspended time, in a concentration can. It's not as hospitable and prepared to life as would be the secret temple which is inside the female body that is a womb which is by far much better equipped physiologically, chemically, and I would say intellectually than our best laboratories for the development of a new human being.

That is the reason why thinking about those things, I was deeply moved when you phoned to me, knowing that Madame, the mother, wanted to rescue babies from this concentration can. And to give to the baby—I would not use term *baby*, it is not perfectly accurate, not good English—would offer to those early human beings, her own flesh, the hospitality that she is the best in the world to give them. And because Mr. Palmer told me on the phone that it had been said that if you, Madame, were not entitled to give this shelter to the baby—to the early human beings (being perfectly correct in what I mean)—you would prefer that they would be enjoying another shelter and not being left inside the concentration can, or destroyed. And I was impressed because it remembered me of an extraordinary trial which has occurred more than two thousand years ago, and I could not believe it could occur again, that two people will discuss whether it's better to have an early human being alive and given to a certain person or another person would prefer the baby not being alive at all. And to the best of my recollection this judgment has been considered as a paragon of justice when Solomon did it. I was not thinking I would come from Paris to speak in Tennessee about a two thousand years old trial. But I realized when you phoned to me, it was the first time it was arising in this earth with a very early human being, because before early human beings were not in our reach, they were protected inside the secret temple. And then I felt it was opportunity that a geneticist was going to tell you what our own science tells us.

If this trial had taken place two years before, I would have stopped because I would have told you all that we knew at that moment. But with your permission, your Honor, I will continue a little further, faster and faster.

THE COURT: Yes.

THE WITNESS: We know much more, since the last two years; we know that the uniqueness of the early human being I was talking at the beginning, which was a statistical certainty (but an inference of all we knew about the frequency of the genes, about the difference between individuals) is now an experimentally demonstrated fact. That has been discovered less than two years ago by Jeffreys in England, the remarkable manipulator of DNA. And Jeffreys invented that he could select a little piece of DNA, of which he could manufacture a lot of it, which is specific of some message in our chromosomes. It is repeated a lot of times in many different chromosomes and which is probably a regulation system. Some indication to do something or do another thing, but not a kitchen recipe, but a precision about what to do.

And because it's only telling the cells that this should work and this should not work, it can assume a lot of tiny change, so that there are so many of those little genes and there are so many little changes in them that we receive from father and from mother an array of those genes that we can realize very simply, you get the DNA, you put it in solution and you have it spread in a special medium. Then you put this special probe made by Jeffreys, and what you see it looks exactly like the bar code that you have probably seen in the supermarket, that is, small lines of different breadth and different distance from each other. If you put that bar code and you read it with an electronic device, it tells the computer what the price of the object and tells a lot of other things.

Well, it's exactly what it tells us that when we look at the DNA bar code, and we detect every individual is different from the next one by its own bar code. And that is not any longer a demonstration by statistical reasoning. So many investigations have been made that we know now that looking at the bar code with his Jeffreys system, the probability that you will find it identical in another person is less than one in a billion. So it's not any longer a theory that each of us is unique. It's now a demonstration as simple as a bar code in the supermarket. It does not tell you the price of human life, it has a difference with supermarket.

The second advance has been that we know now that in one cell we can detect its originality. That has been due to the discovery of a new system which is called PCR, which is becoming extraordinary popular. It started two years ago. You can take a tiny piece of DNA, one molecule taken from one cell, you see how little this is, you can with that technique reproduce it by billions, and when you have enough you can make the analysis of Jeffreys and see again that we have the whole demonstration of uniqueness, not only in a sample taken from the individual, but in one cell, in one nucleus of one individual.

Another is a third discovery which is by far the most important of all, which is that DNA is not as dull as the magnetic tape I was talking before. Nature is imitated by our discoveries, but she has known much more than we have yet discovered. In that sense, that the message written on DNA is written by change of the various bases which come one after the other in that one-meter-long molecule. But now it happens that twenty years ago it was described with certainty that some of the bases of DNA were carrying an extra little piece we call a methyl (which is CH3), which is just hooked on it and change a little of the form of one of the bars of this long scale which is the DNA molecule. Nobody understood what it was meaning. And it's only four years ago (especially by the discovery of Surani) that we have begun to understand that we were up to something extraordinary, which is that those tiny little bits of methyl which are put on the base, cytosine, which is transformed in methyl—cytosine—I'm sorry to be technical, your Honor, but I cannot translate it, it's chemical slang.

THE COURT: I understand.

THE WITNESS: Is exactly comparable to what does an intelligent reader when he wants with a pen to underline, to highlight some passage or to scratch, delete another sentence. That is with the methylation, one gene which is still there is knocked out, put to silence, but if it is demethylated on the next division, on the next cell, then it will speak again.

Now, the basic discovery was that this is possible because this tiny change on the DNA changes the surface of the big groove of the helix of DNA. It is inside this big groove that some molecules, some proteins, will hook on different segments specific of the DNA. It is a kind of language telling to the chromosome: You have to tell this information or for this information, shut up, do not speak this one for the moment. It's very necessary, because there is so many information in our cells that if they were expressing everything, every time, to have the energy spent by one cell would be much more than the energy of our whole body. So it's necessary that we have some silent gene and some gene giving expression, expressed.

Now, the basic discovery is the following, and it is directly related to our discussion: That the DNA carried by the sperm is not underlined (or crossed) by this methylation on the same places which are not equivalent in the DNA chromosomes carried by ovum. During the manufacture of the sperm there are indications, it's penciled, so to speak. It's underlined, you should do that. But on the equivalent gene, on the equivalent chromosome manufactured by the mother, the underline is in a different place, and it underlines something different. So that at the moment the two sets of chromosomes carried by the sperms and the egg are put together, they are not as we believed for years identical. We knew there was a difference with the "X" and "Y" chromosomes, but for the others they were believed to carry the same information; that is not true. Some information is to be read on as coming from the male chromosome, and another information from a chromosome coming from the mother. Now, the reason is that the fertilized egg is the most specialized cell under the sun because it has a special indication underlining segments of DNA which shall be expressed and others that shall not be expressed that no other cell will ever have in the life of this individual.

When it's split in two we know that exchange of information comes from one cell to the other one. When it's split in three it receives information we are an individual. And when it continues progressively, the underlining system is progressively changed so that cells do differentiate, and cells become specialized doing a nail, doing hair, doing skin, doing neurons, doing everything.

And the very thing is that during this process, the expansion of the primary formula which is written in the early human being, nothing is learned but progressively a lot of things are forgotten. The first cell knew more than the three-cell stage, and the three-cell stage knew more than the morula, than the gastrula, than the primitive streak, and the primitive nervous system. In the beginning it was written really not only what is the genetic message we can read in every cell, but it was written the way it should be read from one sequence to another one. Exactly like in the program of a computer, you don't put only the equivalent of the algebraic formula, but you tell to the computer do that; if you get that result, then go at that and continue that program; or if you don't get the result, continue and go to the other program. That is written in the first cell; is progressively forgotten in the other cells of our body.

At the end of the process when the organism has grown up, it produces then its own reproductive cells, it puts the counter to zero again, and hence the rejuvenation. A new life will begin when a female and a male cell will encounter to produce the next generation. So I would say very precisely, your Honor, that two years ago I would not have been able to give you this very simple but extremely valuable information which we have now, beyond any doubt.

I would give you an example of why it's not theoretical. We can manipulate with mice—not me, but my colleagues. And with mice they have been able to make pseudo zygote, that is, to take one egg, expel its own legitimate nucleus and put, for example, two nuclei coming from sperm, so they have diploid cell, a diploid zygote containing only two sets of paternal origin; it fails to grow. They have tried to do it with two maternal original nuclei, that is, two maternal chromosomal cells and no paternal cells. It's diploid; by the old theory it should grow, but it does not. But curiously both of them do something, they don't build a full *imago*, that is, the whole form. But they specialize. If there is only male nuclei, two male nuclei making what is called an androgenote, it produce little cysts which are looking like the membranes and placenta that the child is normally building around himself to make its space and time capsule so that it could take the fluid from the mother vessels. An early zygote containing only male chromosome does only that.

If a zygote contains only chromosomes from female origin, it makes the spare parts. It makes pieces of skin, it makes piece of teeth, it can make a little nail, but all that in a full disorder, not at all constructed it makes the spare parts. We know this directly by experiment in mice done by Surani last year. But we knew that but we could not understood it before.

We knew that already in man, because in man we know that there are what is called dermoid cysts which is a division of a non-fertilized egg inside the ovary of a virgin girl. It cannot grow. It's rare, but it is well known. It will never give a little baby, but it makes the spare parts, teeth, nails, all that mixed in incomprehensible disorder. On the reverse we knew that sometime after apparently normal fertilization the product does not divide correctly but makes cysts, little balls again and again and again, and it's called a mole, *hydatidiformis* mole, and it's very dangerous because it can give the cancer to the pregnant woman.

Now, we have discovered—(not me), you have to know I'm professor, and when I say we, it's all the professors of the world, it's not me. We have discovered that in those *hydatidiformis* moles, there were only paternal chromosomes. There were two sets of paternal chromosomes and the maternal pronuclei had died, we don't know why. So we know by the mice experiments that it is related to methylation of the DNA.

Hence, we know by the human observation, that there is a specialization of information carried by the sperm compared to the information carried by the ovum. And I would say I was wondering, not surprised, but wondering that we were discovering at this extraordinarily tiny level of information built into the chromosomes, that paternal duty was to build the shelter and to make the gathering of the food, to build the hut and the hunting. And that the maternal trick was household and building of the spare parts so the individual can build himself. And it's a kind of admiration that we have for nature that since we have seen in the grown up that the man is going hunting and the mother is doing the kitchen, it is just the same deeply written inside our own chromosomes at the very beginning at the moments the first human constitution is spelled out.

Well, I have abused your kindness, your Honor. I have spoken maybe too much, but I would say to finish that there is no, no difficulty to understand that at the very beginning of life, the genetic information and the molecular structure of the egg, the spirit and the matter, the soul and the body must be that tightly intricated because it's a beginning of the new marvel that we call a human.

It's very remarkable for the geneticist that we use the same word to define an idea coming into our mind and a new human coming into life. We use only one word: *conception*. We conceive an idea, we conceive a baby. And genetics tell us you are not wrong using the same word; because what is conception? It's really giving information written in the matter so that this matter is now not any longer matter but is a new man.

When we come back to the early human beings in the concentration can, I think we have now the proof that there are not spare parts in which we could take at random, they are not experimental material that we could throw away after using it, they are not commodities we could freeze and defreeze at our own will, they are not property that we could exchange against anything. And if I understand well the present case and if I can say a word as geneticist, I would say: An early human being inside this suspended time which is the can cannot be the property of anybody because it's the only one in the world to have the property of building himself. And I would say that science has a very simple conception of man; as soon as he has been conceived, a man is a man.

Q. Dr. Lejeune, suppose that—as a hypothetical question, but suppose that we had heard testimony in this hearing that indicated that each mom and each dad contribute identically the same to the embryo, and that there is no differentiation between their contributions, could you tell us what your opinion is about whether or not cells are differentiated?

A. It's difficult to answer that because once you know something in science, it's very difficult to tell what you would think if you were not knowing it. If the paternal and maternal chromosomal share of the baby was the same, we wouldn't have any idea how this differentiation of cells do occur, so if I had testified two years ago, I would have said that the mystery of cell differentiation was complete, and we did not know where it was written. Now we begin to know where it's written. It's the only difference, but it's a great difference that we begin to know. It tells us definitely that what was an implication that it must be written in the first cell (this type of differentiation must occur at this time and at the other time another differentiation should occur). We knew it should have been written, but we did not know at all how it was.

Q. Okay. And so you testified at great length about the differentiation.

A. Yeah.

Q. And you did that for what purpose?

A. For the purpose of understanding how from an apparently undifferentiated cell which is the one cell of the fertilized zygote, the full *imago* can emerge. If science cannot say anything about the mechanism of it, it just remains a pure constitution but no knowledge about it. It's the reason why I wanted to put on record those new findings about the methylation of DNA, because it proved that the implication which was as all of genetics, that differentiation is, so to speak, prewritten in the first cell, is now having an understandable physical support. Now, it cannot be said that the first cell is a non-differentiated cell. It must be said now the first cell is knowing how to differentiate the progeny, the cell progeny.

Q. Okay. And for me to understand —

A. To make it clearer, if I am looking at the mass of cell growing, I know by my own experience in my lab for twenty years that never a baby will form itself in our bottles because we are growing cells taken from the body. On the contrary we know that if the cell which is dividing is a fertilized zygote, a new individual is just now beginning to emerge.

Q. What ethical considerations do you have about freezing?

A. I think love is the contrary of chilly. Love is warmth, and life needs good temperature. So I would consider that the best we can do for early human beings is to have them in their normal shelter, not in the fridge. The fridge is not a second choice, I would say it's a third choice. And typically I would not be surprised that in a few years from now, this long way outside the female body which is artificial insemination and this long stay in concentration can will be considered as not very efficient. It will be much better to make graft of the tubes to repair the difficulty of the tubal incapacity, or to use antibiotics—new antibiotics to prevent special difficulty with the mucosa of the tubes, or find chemicals which will help find why certain couples, although they have normal production of cells, cannot manage to get fertilization, or to get implantation. It's surely some chemical thing which is not yet discovered which will be the real solution. Then

I would consider that the extracorporeal fertilization, it's, so to speak, an emergency proposal of medicine on the present stage of medicine, but it's not good treatment. The good treatment is yet to be found in each of the cases. It's not the final answer, so to speak, not at all. That is my feeling, but it's a feeling.

Q. Within your knowledge, Doctor, can you tell us what we know and what we can tell about these human beings from three cells forward? What knowledge do we gain and at what rate do we gain it? Do you understand my question?

A. No.

Q. Okay. We have heard testimony that at three weeks you have got this, the nervous system starts at this stage—

A. Yeah.

Q. This starts when and it's been confusing, because we have tried to eliminate—we tried to identify body parts, we're thinking in terms, and you come to us with a different perspective. Can you tell us once again what it is we have and how it progresses in development?

A. Well, from the very beginning we have a embryo. We have first a zygote and a two-cell embryo and then a three-cell embryo and then a four-cell embryo, and then eight, and sixteen, and all the power of two. This embryo, growing progressively, is inside the *zona pellucida*, and suddenly at around six days or seven days it begins to "hatch." The *zona pellucida* is, in fact, the protection, or privacy, so that if they are twins, for example, they will not mix together because each of them is in its own *zona pellucida*.

At the moment the embryo begins to hatch and make trophoblast which will anchor itself on the mucosa, there is already so much commitments we cannot see. There is already so much committed to build the individual that it will not mix with a possible twin. Otherwise, in species in which you have a lot of pups in a litter of five, ten, like in kittens or in dogs, if they were not protected, each of them at the beginning in their own plastic bag (in their own *zona pellucida*), they would not make different animals, they would mix and make a kind of chimera. But when it's so well committed, when all the cells are so well committed to continue to cooperate with each other, then nature has invented that embryo will hatch and rupture the *zona pellucida* and begin to anchor on the uterus.

The second step, we can describe around twelve days after fertilization; that is the very beginning of the little line which cells begin to draw on the embryo; this little line will progressively become a kind of *gouttiere*—I don't know the word in English—and finally will close itself in a tube, and it will be the beginning of the neural tube.

Then well, let's say, what I should say more? I will describe the whole development of the *imago*, let's say at three weeks, the cardiac tubes will begin to beat, so that the heart is beginning to beat three weeks after fertilization. And progressively you will reach the end of the embryonic period at two months after fertilization. At that moment the little fellow will be just size of my thumb. And it's because of that that all the mothers telling fairy tales to the children are speaking about Tom Thumb story because it's a true story. Therefore, each of us has been a Tom Thumb in the womb of the mother and women have always known that there was a kind of underground country, a kind of vaulted shelter, with a kind of red light and curious noise in which very tiny humans were having a very curious and marvelous life. That is the story of Tom Thumb.

Well, after Tom Thumb is visible, that is, two months of age, it has two centimeters and a half from the crown to the rump, and if I had it—if I had him on my fist, you would not see that I have something, but if I was opening my hand you would see the tiny man with hands, with fingers, with toes. Everything is there, the brain is there and will continue to grow.

It's from that moment which is two months after fertilization, that we don't call any longer human being embryos, we call them fetuses. And that is very true to change the name just because it tells a very plain evidence: Nobody in the world looking for the first time at a Tom Thumb bag, looking at an embryo of two months of a chimpanzee, of a gorilla, of an orangutan, or of a man, nobody in the world would make a mistake just looking at him. It's obvious this one is a chimpanzee, this one is an orangutan, this one is gorilla, this one is a man.

The reason why we change the name, and we call it fetus, it means only something to be carried because the full form is already present. But the man was there before everybody could tell the difference with a chimp. For example, if we were taking one cell—I would not do that because it's dangerous for the being, but if we were taking one cell of a four-cell embryo, it would probably survive and compensate. We know it in mouse. Now, let's take one cell of a chimpanzee embryo, of a human embryo, of a gorilla embryo and give it to one of my students in the Certificate of Cytogenetics in Paris, and if he cannot tell you this one is a human being, this one is a chimpanzee being, this one is a gorilla being, he would fail his exam; it's as simple as that.

Q. When you see the development of three cells —

A. Yeah.

Q. And if we used the most intricate computers, let's say, that would be used in our space program, NASA we call it, could those computers be programmed to keep up with what is going on?

A. No, totally not. The amount of information which is inside the zygote, which would if spelled out and put in a computer tell the computer how to calculate what will happen next, this amount of information is that big that nobody can measure it.

I have to explain that very simply. You have the two meters of DNA, one coming from father, one coming from mother, that it means ten to the eleven bits of information, just to spell out what is written on this DNA. If you add the subscript that I was talking about methylation, then it will increase this number by ten to the power four or to the power five. Thus, we will go very soon, just for the DNA, at ten to the fifteen. It's an enormous number. To give you an idea, just to print letter by letter all what it is written in the DNA of a fertilized egg, you would need, writing G, C, T, A, and all the string of symbols, you would need five times the Encyclopedia Britannica just to spell out the DNA, five times Encyclopedia Britannica. But nobody could read it. You could fit it into the computer. But now you would have to take care of all the molecules that are inside the cytoplasm which will recognize the message, which will send a message to the next cell. And to spell out this amount of information which is absolutely necessary (otherwise no life would be possible), I think you would need a thousand, a million times more bits of information. No computer in the world would have a storage enough just to fill the amount of data. Now, to tell to the computer the algorithm to use it, nobody knows how to do it. You have to realize that this enormous information which makes a man is enormous compared to the information which makes a computer, because it's a man who has made the computer; it's not the computer which has made the man.

MR. CHRISTENBERRY: You may ask him. I would like to interject at first if the Court—while it's fresh on the Court's mind, would have any questions of the doctor. He's used to facing a judge after he's told his side of the story, and sometimes we do that in our system.

THE COURT: I have no questions at this point.

MR. CLIFFORD: Thank you, your Honor.

CROSS EXAMINATION BY MR. CLIFFORD:

Q. *Bon jour*, Dr. Lejeune.

A. *Merci.*

Q. Now, in genetics, I would take it, it has been believed on the theoretical level, all of the genetic material, all of the information as you referred to it was in the zygote, that has been believed theoretically for a very long time?

A. No doubt.

Q. And that what you have described to us at such length today has been the working out of the precise mechanism of how that works?

A. In a sense, yes, but it's a little change that previously it was an inference and now we begin to have a demonstration. For a scientist it makes a lot of difference.

Q. Of course. But if I had come to you, Dr. Lejeune, ten years ago, and I had said, please help me with my genetics, Doctor, do you believe that all of the information that's necessary for the development and maturation of a chicken—

A. Yeah.

Q. Is contained in that zygotic cell we first see in the egg—

A. Yeah.

Q. Would you have told me that you believed that?

A. Well, to be perfectly correct, I would say I believe it; now I would say I know it. That's a small difference.

Q. But I take it it would be true that, again, ten years ago had I asked you this question about the chicken that your level of conviction about all that information being in the zygotic cell would have been very high?

A. Yes, pretty.

Q. And certainly if in genetics we had discovered that some information was coming into cells from some other source than the genetic material and having an impact, we would have all been stunned, scientific world would have been stunned?

A. Yeah, yeah.

Q. Now then, you described at great length this morning, the precise nature of the development of embryos as far as the mechanics of the genes and chromosomes and information that is passed from each gamete into that zygote, and you, of course, described it as an incredibly complicated procedure.

A. Uh-huh (affirmative).

Q. I take it that your questions, you were answering specifically about human embryos, zygotes, sperm, ova, but I take it that is also true of chimpanzees, gorillas, mice, they are—in those species it's also a very complicated fascinating complex mechanism?

A. Yes, but not exactly the same mechanism.

Q. Certainly. I think I have read somewhere, and I'm sure if I'm not right you'll correct me, that genetically as far as the chromosomes, as far as the contents of the DNA in the chromosomes, for instance, man, *Homo sapiens*, and the higher mammals, particularly the gorillas, chimpanzees—help me look for that species.

A. Orangutan.

Q. There is a remarkable similarity?

A. Well, it depends what you remark. You can remark the similarity, or you can remark the differences. Arid difference is incredibly interesting. I don't know where you want to ask me.

Q. Well, I have heard it said or read that approximately ninety-eight percent of the genetic material that is found in a chimpanzee or gorilla is identical to what may be found in a human being.

A. It has been written, and it has been written by statistical calculation of the DNA but not about the meaning of it. Now, what makes ninety percent similarity in the number of words in two different texts? They can mean something very different by the way the sentences are made. It's what makes the difference between the species.

Q. But there is a similarity in the DNA?

A. Oh, yes, exactly like the similarity in the fact they have two hands like us, not the same thumb, but they have hands, we have feet, but they are the most similar to us, no doubt. It's no surprise that the DNA also has some similarity.

Q. But the same basic process that we observe in human beings we also observe in chimpanzees?

A. Oh, yes.

Q. Mice?

A. Mice, I would not go that far but partly.

Q. Mice have zygotes?

A. Oh, yes, I mean—I want to make clear when we speak about basic mechanism we have to know what we mean by basic. For example, I told you the enormous importance of methylation of the DNA we discovered those years. But, for example, *Drosophila* does not methylate the DNA.

Q. That's the fruit fly?

A. That's the fruit fly but it's a very complex organism. It makes a differentiation of cells that makes me believe that with methylation we have unveiled one of the tricks used by nature, but there are other tricks we are still using, we men, that were sufficient to build a *Drosophila* but would not be sufficient to build the human being. I would not agree that basic mechanism are the same in the whole living system. Surely it's much more complicated to build a human being, to determinate on one cell the wiring of his brain so that he will some day invent machine to help his own brain to understand the law of the universe. There is something peculiar to the human beings compared to others, you know. I will tell you one thing, very simple: I'm traveling a lot, and as far as I can I visit two points which are very important for me when I go in a new town: One is the university and other is the zoological garden. In the university I have often seen very grave professors asking themselves whether after all their children when they were very young were not animals, but I have never seen in a zoological garden a congress of chimpanzees asking themselves whether their children when they are grown up will become universitarians. I feel there is a difference somewhere.

Q. Doctor, I forgot to ask you a couple of questions about your expertise, and please pardon me for having to come back, but I take it from your testimony when Mr. Christenberry was asking you questions that you have not worked in the field of what is called in this country in-vitro fertilization?

A. No.

Q. I believe in France there is a different term for that.

A. No, it's called also *fecundation in vitro.*

Q. But you have not been involved in any in-vitro fertilization clinics?

A. No.

Q. You have not been asked to advise in-vitro fertilization clinics on matters of genetics or anything else?

A. Not directly, but I have advised a lot of my patients who consider whether they should have or not this type of investigation.

Q. I suppose I should ask you this, I understand in-vitro fertilization is done in France?

A. Oh, yes.

Q. How long has this procedure been carried out in your country?

A. Well, I think Amanda has been six years, now, six years and a half, she was the first test-tube baby in Paris. I think she is six years, seven years maybe.

Q. Let me see, Dr. Lejeune, if I understand the point you are making this morning. It is your belief as a geneticist, that all the information that is necessary to create a human being, a unique individual human being, we could go in and find in a nucleus of a zygote?

A. No, I never said that. In the zygote I would say, not in the nucleus. You need the nucleus and whole cytoplasm. The zygote cannot be reduced to the magnetic tape. We have also to have the tape recorder working.

Q. We can take if we wished on a perhaps philosophical scientific experiment here, we could take a zygote, look at it, look at the DNA, look at the other structures in that one cell and assuming that we had the knowledge to be able to do it, tell everything about that human being?

A. I would say yes, beside accident, which cannot be predicted, but I would say no machine is big enough to put in it this information, it is purely hypothetical.

Q. Right.

A. It's not practical.

Q. We're engaging on a philosophical experiment.

A. To be frank and to give you my belief, I'm not sure we'll be any time able to build a machine big enough to do that job. There is no evidence about that.

Q. Dr. Lejeune, then theoretically—

A. Otherwise this machine would be a fertilized egg itself.

Q. But if we had such a machine on our philosophical experiment, we could look into the zygote, and we could tell what color hair this person would have?

A. No doubt.

Q. What color eyes this person could have?

A. Yes.

Q. Could we look into the zygote and, either in the structure or chromosome or DNA, and tell what language the person would speak?

A. I don't believe so, sir, because language is a basic phenomenon built in. We could say, in your example, theoretical example, this being will be able to speak, but he will speak Japanese if he is in Tokyo. But we could say conversely with your same system, looking at a chimpanzee first cell, this being will never speak.

Q. Could we look into the zygote, into the genes of the chromosomes, into the DNA structure and tell whether this individual would like the music of Beethoven?

A. Partly, yes, sir, because we could in your hypothesis be sure that he is perfectly normal, and if he is perfectly normal he would like Beethoven.

Q. Dr. Lejeune, do you intend to investigate to find the defective chromosomes for those who do not like Beethoven?

A. No, no, but you were asking me about normality.

Q. Could we look into the zygote, into the chromosomes, DNA, into the balance of the structure, and tell whether this individual would grow up to be a person of liberal or conservative persuasion?

A. Well, even looking at the grown-up I cannot tell that, sir.

Q. Of course, as you realize, Professor Lejeune, I'm trying to make, I guess, a philosophical point, and that is while some information, a great deal obviously of information is contained in that zygote, that there would obviously be things we could not detect with our philosophical machine about the individual when he or she was twenty, forty or sixty?

A. Uh-huh (affirmative).

Q. Dr. Lejeune, let me come I guess to what is the heart of the matter here and the heart of your testimony. You mentioned using the word *conception* and defining it in two different ways, defining it as the point where a zygote comes into existence and the point where we have a thought, and really would you agree with me, Dr. Lejeune, that what we're concerned about in this case and in the great debate about human life are definitions? How do we define a human being?

A. Oh, yes.

Q. Now, of course, when you define a human being, what we're assuming there is that a human being has certain rights, whether God-given rights or legal rights?

A. That is not what defines a human being.

Q. Of course not. I understand. But I take it and I will ask you directly, Dr. Lejeune: You have referred to the zygote and the embryo as quote "early human beings."

A. Yeah.

Q. Do you regard an early human being as having the same moral rights as a later human being such as myself?

A. You have to excuse me, I'm very, very direct. As far as your nature is concerned, I cannot see any difference between the early human being you were and the late human being you are, because in both case, you were and you are a member of our species. What defines a human being is: He belongs to our species. So an early one or a late one has not changed from its species to another species. It belongs to our kin. That is a definition. And I would say very precisely that I have the same respect, no matter the amount of kilograms and no matter the amount of differentiation of tissues.

Q. Dr. Lejeune, let me make sure I understand what you are telling us, that the zygote should be treated with the same respect as an adult human being?

A. I'm not telling you that because I'm not in a position of knowing that. I'm telling you, he is a human being, and then it is a justice who will tell whether this human being has the same rights as the others. If you make difference between human beings, that is on your own to prove the reasons why you make that difference. But as a geneticist, you ask me whether this human being is a human, and I would tell you that because he is a being and being human, he is a human being.

Q. And I take it you would believe from your testimony today that it is morally very wrong to intentionally kill a zygote?

A. I think it's no good, it's killing a member of our species.

Q. And it would be the same as if we were to kill twenty years later the person, human being, that the zygote would become?

A. It's difficult to tell because you ask me a justice question; I'm a biologist.

Q. Now, but those are your beliefs?

A. My belief is that it's no good to kill a member of our kin, very simple belief.

Q. There is not much difference to you between whether it's at the zygote level, the fetus level?

A. There is a great difference as they have not the same age. Some of them are very youthful ones, others are old ones. But it doesn't make for me a great difference, in the true sense of the fact it is discarding a member of my species. It's the only reason why I don't kill people, it's because they are human. Otherwise, some of them—some difficulty in life . . .

Q. Dr. Lejeune, you, of course, are a scientist, and I'm sure that in the large part, you base your convictions and feelings upon your knowledge of genetics and other sciences. Will you concede, Dr. Lejeune, there are other very distinguished scientists, men who are as learned as you, who have thought and who have access to the same scientific information that you have, who come to a different conclusion?

A. About what?

Q. About the moral rights or moral duty to the zygote.

A. Oh, in that case yes, but not about the fact it's a human being or not.

Q. I understand that.

A. But that's the point.

Q. I understand that. There are even, I believe, individuals in your own country who differ with your view of what ethical duty is owed to the zygote.

A. Well, I think in France we are divided in forty million opinions about that.

Q. But you do recognize there are men in your own country of great learning who differ with your view on the ethics of the embryo and zygotic levels?

A. Oh, that's obvious.

Q. I believe, Dr. Lejeune, in the earlier—or I'd say slightly mid-nineteen eighties, your country set up a commission to study the ethical concerns raised by the technology of in-vitro fertilization. Are you aware of the national commission?

A. Well, you can call it a national commission, it's specially appointed by the president of France, so all the people have been nominated by the president. It's a presidential thing. It's not really a national thing. It's called national, but it's not elected so it's not representative at all.

Q. Well, I believe it was called national commission.

A. They have called them national commission, but you have to know they are not representative. They are not elected by bodies.

Q. Were you on that committee?

A. No, and I can tell you why, because I'm a member of the *Academie des Sciences Morales et Politiques*, moral and political sciences, and normally a member of this academy should have been appointed ex officio. Deliberately in the constitution, the by-laws of this committee, our academy was not put on it because they knew that the *Academie des Sciences Morales et*

Politiques would appoint me. Just an interesting phenomenon.

Q. So you feel—

A. I don't feel anything about it. It's just a fact. I don't feel anything.

Q. You believe you were intentionally kept off this committee?

A. I believe that our academy was kept off, no doubt.

Q. Since they knew that it would be you that was appointed, you were intentionally kept off?

A. That is a scientific hypothesis, not demonstrated.

Q. But you do, I take it, recognize that the members of the national commission that were appointed were distinguished persons in their fields?

A. I have never seen somebody in a committee who is not distinguished, sir.

Q. And regarding those individuals, even if you disagree with them, I take it you would recognize their integrity?

A. Case by case.

Q. Case by case.

A. Case by case.

Q. Do you know all the members of the committee?

A. No.

Q. But you would, in general, agree they are persons of integrity and learning?

A. Case by case.

Q. Are you familiar with the report of the national commission?

A. Yes, I have read it.

Q. You have read it?

A. Yes.

Q. The report of your national commission expresses some very grave reservations about the technique we know here as cryopreservation. Are you familiar with that?

A. Uh-huh (affirmative).

Q. Let me ask you this, Dr. Lejeune: Do you share those reservations about cryopreservation?

A. I have many reservations. Probably it's not very good.

Q. We heard testimony from Dr. Shivers, who was the embryologist who worked in this case, that with cryopreservation there was a statistical loss of the frozen embryos in the range of, I believe he said, fifteen to thirty percent.

A. He's a better specialist about this attrition percent than I am.

Q. So that you can expect, therefore, by the rules of statistics if we freeze one hundred pre-embryos, and we come back to thaw them at any point, we know the odds are very, very high we'll only have seventy, seventy-five or eighty?

A. Uh-huh (affirmative).

Q. We knew that before we put them in the Frigidaire?

A. Yes.

Q. Would you regard that as an intentional killing of embryos?

A. No, but I would consider that it's making the embryo running a risk, and whether this risk was in the best interest of the embryo or not is an open question. I explain. When we do an intervention in a baby for a heart disease, in some intervention we know that around twenty percent of them will be killed by the intervention. And in this case the intervention is made only if we know if we don't operate the child will be killed by the disease at ninety-nine percent of probability. Then we say in the real interests of this patient the best for him is to operate even if the operation is still dangerous, the danger is much greater if we don't operate. That is a way you can make indeed some choices in medicine which are dangerous but which are, in fact, the best that you can do in the interest of this particular patient.

Now, in the case of an embryo, I am not sure it is in his own interest that this choice is made.

Q. In fact, it's made in a choice that as Dr. Shivers and Dr. King testified previously, that it merely gives the woman a better chance since she won't have to go through the stimulated cycle having shots and medication, hormones injected into her, it simply gives her a better chance of becoming pregnant. You're aware of that?

A. I am aware of that.

Q. So in cryopreservation we know that we are going to kill ten, twenty, thirty percent of these early human beings merely so the woman has a better chance of getting pregnant?

A. That would be one of the reservations that I would have, but I dislike you say you kill. It's not killing.

Q. If we were to take the members, the individuals seated in the jury box, and I were to have a room I could put them in where we would know that thirty percent of them would come out dead, would you not agree I would be guilty of murder?

A. Well, it depends, sir, because if the room you were talking about were a shelter during a bombing time and if remaining in that room all of them will be dead, but in the shelter some of them will survive, even if thirty percent of them will be dead, you did well. So it depends on the reason why you did it.

Q. What if I did it not to take them out of a position of greater harm but merely for the benefit of some person other than themselves, not one of them but Mr. Palmer?

A. I suppose he would refuse you do it, I'm sure.

Q. You recognize the ethical and moral dilemma I'm raising, of course?

A. No, I don't recognize it, sir.

Q. You don't?

A. No, because you use the word *killing*. And if you take an embryo which has been frozen and you put him briskly at normal temperature so that he will die, you are killing the embryo. If you are freezing the embryo you are not trying to kill him; if I understand what you have in your mind to is to help the embryo surviving so he could be implanted in the womb of the mother. So your technique is not good because you lose part of them, but you are not killing. And I would not say that my colleagues who are freezing embryos are killers. It's not true. Otherwise, maybe it's because I don't understand English, but I would not use the word *kill*.

Q. The national commission in its report used a term which in English is *supernumerary*?

A. Yeah.

Q. Referring to supernumerary embryos, referring particularly to cryopreservation, embryos which are not to be used with a particular patient, woman, who has undergone WF. Are you familiar with that term, first of all?

A. I know that term, and it's a wrong term. Can you tell me a man who is supernumerary?

Q. Maybe just a lawyer.

A. I don't believe that, as a man he is not supernumerary. Maybe—I'm not saying anything.

Q. But that is the term that is used in the report of the national commission?

A. Yes, but it is a very misleading term, exactly the same thing as pre-embryo. You change the name because you will change your behavior, and I dislike that. I like to call a cat a cat, and a man a man. It's Wendell Holmes who said a man is a man is a man.

Q. And a dog a dog and chicken a chicken?

A. No, but "a man is a man is a man," is a saying in your country.

Q. Well, rather at this point debating whether the term was wise or not, I'm asking if that was the term that was used.

A. Right.

Q. Now, as I think I asked you and you told me awhile ago, the French commission did have reservations about the whole process of cryopreservation, because, of course, it leads to the precise problem that we have in this case. Of course, you know that regular IVF the woman is implanted or pre-embryos—excuse me, the embryos are inserted within forty-eight hours?

A. As soon as you can, yes.

Q. Whereas with a cryopreserved embryo, it might be six months, it might be a year. In fact, I believe that you are aware that the French guidelines provide for a year for the first child, recommend that a cryopreserved embryo should not be saved longer than twelve months for the first child?

A. Could I tell you because you speak about what is said in French that this committee is consultative. It means that what he says as guidelines is for himself.

Q. But these are the guidelines published by the national commission that was appointed by your government—

A. It's consultative. It has no law, no force; just an opinion.

Q. But you are aware that the commission recommended one year for the first child?

A. Yes.

Q. And then with an extension of an additional twelve months if a second child was desired?

A. I don't follow you.

Q. One question that was raised in the commission was how long you should keep a cryopreserved embryo.

A. Yes.

Q. Now, and the committee recommended that it should not exceed twelve months without very special circumstances and without a great deal of thought by people concerned with the ethical dilemma of IVF, do you recall that?

A. I know about that, but I don't see the meaning.

Q. I'm just asking you about the report at this point.

A. Yes. Nobody knows from where it was coming, the time of one year. Out of the air?

Q. Now, the French commission recognized that one of the dilemmas that was posed by cryopreservation again was the open-ended time, time during which, as in this case, things could change, is that correct?

A. I have to be very precise, I don't know by heart the whole document you are talking about.

Q. I'm not going to ask you to quote it. But let me ask you this: Are you aware that the national commission of France that spoke on this subject recommended that in the case where the project of the couple, that is, the IVF project of this couple is abandoned in the meantime, and that meantime refers to cryopreservation being used or is unfeasible because, for example, of the separation of the couple, the only solution retained by the committee by way of the least evil consist in the destruction of the embryos with the reservation of the possibility of donation for research?

A. I'm not aware of that at all, sir, because the consultative committee said it would not give any indication because they have not reached any opinion. I don't know what document you are talking about, but the one I have read was not this one. If you talk about this document, the opinions saying that it's better to kill the frozen embryos, it's just in my opinion wrong, I disagree with it.

MR. CLIFFORD: Your Honor, may I approach the witness?
THE COURT: You may.

Q. Let me show you a page here which unfortunately for me is in French.

A. That's good for me.

Q. And ask if you could read the title of the document?

A. (Reading in French.)

Q. Could you—

A. I'll try to make a translation. Advice concerning research on human embryos in-vitro and their utilization for medical and scientific purposes.

Q. Could you continue to read the page? If you would rather not—

A. Well, what interest?

Q. Just the headings.

A. Recommendation to the use of in-vitro fertilization as answer to infertility—it's very long.

Q. Well, that is, in fact, the report of the national commission, is it not?

A. Well, I'm sorry, sir, but it's not printed. It's something made on a computer. I don't see any important document there because it's—probably it has been a project of it, but it has not been published as a final advice because as I know, what I have heard on television, they said they have not reached an opinion on that. I'm sorry, but it doesn't matter anyway. It's a consultative party.

Q. I'm somewhat surprised by that answer, Dr. Lejeune, because I'm given to understand—you can correct me here—in December of 1986, a committee of distinguished French scientists made their report to the government. The report was started 1983.

A. No, no, there is no final advice given by this body on this particular problem. They have discussed it, and they said we will continue to discuss it, as far as I know.

Q. As far as you know?

A. Uh-huh (affirmative).

Q. You are not familiar with the national commission report?

A. When it is published, yes, I read it, but that is not published matter. I don't see where you want to go with this question.

Q. In fact, Dr. Lejeune, will you agree with me, sir, that there are distinguished, learned men and women in your own country of France who take the view that when a couple separates or is divorced that any embryos that may be in cryopreservation should be discarded or destroyed?

A. That there exists people thinking that, no doubt, because if they say that it's probably because they think it. But it does not prove they're right.

Q. Of course, not. Of course, not. And, of course, I take it because you have your feelings, you would concede that it does not prove that you are right?

A. On that, I would not agree entirely with you.

Q. Okay. All right. Would you agree with me, Dr. Lejeune, that really, of course, we're talking about what will become in this court a legal question?

A. Yeah, partly.

Q. And that legal question is what quote "rights," if any, an embryo should have legally?

A. Disagree with that. I'm not thinking about the rights of the embryos; I'm thinking about the duty of the parents and of society. Duty is a different thing.

Q. Let's talk about duty because that is a word that courts can understand. You believe, in fact, there is a duty, and a strong duty, to bring, or attempt to bring an embryo to term and birth?

A. The embryos have been frozen for that purpose.

Q. I'm not so much talking about the particular seven embryos in this case, but any embryo that's been produced by IVF or in-vitro fertilization.

A. If it has been produced, it has been produced in the view that it could be put somewhere in which it could be developed, that is the womb.

Q. So you would believe that the man has a duty to bring it to life, bring it to birth rather, is that correct?

A. What man?

Q. This man, the man who is the donor of the sperm.

A. Yeah.

Q. That he has a duty, a moral duty to bring it to term?

A. Yes.

Q. And you would believe that the woman has such a duty?

A. I would believe that if she was not feeling having that duty, she would not have accepted the beginning of the process.

Q. Now, you, of course, are best known for your discovery of the chromosome connected with Down's syndrome?

A. That is long ago.

Q. You have researched since that point other conditions or diseases, abnormal conditions which relate to the chromosomes that are passed on by heredity, is that correct?

A. Yeah.

Q. If I understand what you also told us this morning, it is possible to tell at the zygote level whether—

A. Not at the zygote level.

Q. At the embryo level?

A. Yes, and late embryo.

Q. Late embryo level whether or not this early human being will suffer from Down's syndrome?

A. Oh, yes, yes.

Q. And as—

A. In fact, it's essentially for a fetus. It is after two months.

Q. But there is no reason that you know of, I take it that we could not at some point in the not very distant future even make that diagnosis in the embryo level?

A. In some future, might not.

Q. I take it from your testimony, Dr. Lejeune, you would believe that even if the embryo, that early human being, was going to suffer from Down's syndrome or some other very serious condition or abnormality, that it would still be the duty of the mother and the father to bring it to term?

A. I would say the duty is not to kill, and that duty is universal. And I would say that if by technique I was looking at the chromosomes of this baby, and I see the chromosomes abnormal, say for example, he has a trisomy twenty-one, I would say that this is the disease. But if I look at the other forty-six chromosomes that are normal I would see the mankind of the baby. And I don't condemn a member of my kin.

Q. You would believe that the donors of that embryo would have a moral imperative, a duty to bring that—

A. Not to kill the embryo.

Q. That early being into a later stage of human being?

A. Not to kill him.

Q. Now, let me drop back down to a bit more normal level of questions, Dr. Lejeune. Bear with me. Let's take an embryo in general, just statements that we can make about all embryos that would be true. That there is obviously a genetic contribution both by the woman and by the man?

A. Yes, there is a contribution by the father and by the mother.

Q. By the father and by the mother?

A. Yeah.

Q. And without the contribution of either there would be no embryo?

A. Correct.

Q. So on that sense the contributions of the mother and contribution of the father—

A. Are both necessary.

Q. Are equal?

A. No, they are not equal. They are different, but they are both necessary.

Q. Both—

A. Necessary, absolutely.

Q. And now let's talk about a particular embryo, early human being, and let's look at this early human being when it's became a later human being. Obviously, as far as the genetic makeup of this particular individual, it might be, in fact, more strongly influenced by the mother's contribution, at least in some areas, or might be more strongly influenced by the father's contribution.

A. Who knows?

Q. Who knows. And, of course, unless we were to examine it, we wouldn't know.

A. Uh-huh (affirmative).

Q. And certainly you are not in this court saying that women contribute more genetic material?

A. In fact, I'm obliged to say, yes, they contribute more genetic material. For example, all the DNA on the mitochondria is coming from the mother, not from the father. Makes a little difference. It's a fact.

Q. It's a fact?

A. It's a fact.

Q. But it's also a fact without both contributions —

A. They are both necessary, no doubt.

Q. But you are not here today saying, Dr. Lejeune, that the reason, the sole reason that Mrs. Davis should win this case and prevail is because her DNA contribution may have been slightly more than Mr. Davis' DNA contribution?

A. I don't understand your question. I cannot see how you can solve a judicial problem with DNA contributions.

Q. You are saying that it's your opinion that these embryos should be allowed to develop in this young lady because you believe they're early human beings?

A. I do believe they are early human beings, and I have been told that their mother offered them shelter. Who could refuse that?

Q. But not because of DNA contribution?

A. Because they're her own flesh.

Q. Well, they're his own flesh, too, aren't they?

A. Yes.

Q. And obviously he will be their father forever, for the rest of his life if there are children?

A. (Witness nods head in the affirmative).

Q. You will not deny that would have an effect?

A. I would not deny anything.

Q. I take it, Dr. Lejeune, therefore, if you believed that a embryo was not a human being as that term is used in ethical or legal or moral or philosophical or religious way that your view of this case may well be different?

A. Totally. If I was convinced that those early human beings are, in fact, piece of properties, well, property can be discarded, there is no interest for me as a geneticist. But if they are human beings, what they are, then they cannot be considered as property. They need custody.

Q. What it really turns on is what philosophically, ethically, legally that embryo may be. In your mind, sir, you have come to the very firm conviction that the early embryo or that the embryo is a human being, early human being, as you described it?

A. Yes.

Q. And you do recognize in other men's minds, after long and deep thought, learned men, they come to the opposite conclusion you do?

A. No, I don't agree with that.

Q. You don't agree with that?

A. I have not yet seen any scientist coming to the opinion that it is a property. It is what is the case. It's whether they are property that can be discarded, or whether they're human being who must be given to custody. That is it. You ask my question, I answer precisely; I have never heard one of my colleagues—we differ on opinion of many things, but I have never heard one of them telling me or telling to any other that a frozen embryo was the property of somebody, that it could be sold, that it could be destroyed like a property, never. I never heard it.

Q. Just so I understand what you're telling us, I take it, Dr. Lejeune, from your testimony that you would be opposed to abortion?

A. Oh, I dislike to kill anybody. That is very true, sir.

Q. You would believe that abortion should not be legal?

A. That is another point which is different. I think abortion is killing people, and I think in a good jurisdiction would make those killing people become rare. You cannot prevent everything.

Q. I take it, again, your basis of that belief would be that the fetus or embryo is an early human being?

A. Exactly. If it was a tooth, I would not worry about it.

Q. Finally, Dr. Lejeune, I'd like to thank you very much first for coming here to Maryville, Tennessee, to share your scientific and philosophical views with the court. I hope that you enjoy your stay and that your trip back is enjoyable. I have only one final question for you. Okay? What is this?

A. Well, from here I suppose it's an egg, but I'm not sure.

Q. Let me get a little closer.

A. It looks like an egg.

Q. It's an egg?

A. It looks like.

MR. CLIFFORD: Thank you, Doctor, I thought you were going to tell me it was an early chicken.

THE WITNESS: Oh—

MR. CLIFFORD: I have no further questions.

THE WITNESS: Your Honor.

THE COURT: You may respond, if you wish.

THE WITNESS: Yes, I would respond to that because I have never pretended that I could see through a shell. I don't know if it has been fertilized so I cannot know whether it's an early chicken.

Q. All right. Let's talk about the difference for a moment. If I had in this hand a live chicken, would you agree with me if I were to take it and squeeze its head that it would feel pain?

A. Oh, probably.

Q. That it will be frightened?

A. Yes.

Q. And it would suffer psychological, if you can use that term with a chicken, stress?

A. I'm not competent in psychology, you told me, and especially not about chickens.

Q. But if I take this egg and assuming it is fertilized—I wouldn't really do this, Jay—but if I were to crush it in my hand, this egg would not feel pain, it would not be aware in the slightest of what was happening to it?

A. Yeah. But it would be still a chicken and only a chicken.

Q. I thought you told me it was an egg?

A. You told me it was a chicken.

MR. CLIFFORD: No further questions.

(A brief discussion was held off the record.)

CROSS EXAMINATION BY MR. TAYLOR:

Q. Dr. Lejeune, I have just a very few questions. You testified earlier that in the case of freezing human embryos, the temperature is lowered only to, I think, a hundred and eighty or ninety degrees below centigrade, is that correct?

A. Yes, generally.

Q. And because that is not absolute zero there are still certain processes that continue within those embryos?

A. Very slowly.

Q. And because of that, it is your opinion that life or the processes are not suspended completely, and therefore the embryo continues to age or develop, is that right?

A. No, it does not continue to develop, but it can age in the sense of losing some properties because of the agitation of the molecule and not being able to repair it. It's the reason why if you freeze cells, ordinary cells in tissue culture, and if you thaw them, after one month you will get ninety percent groove, after ten years you will get fifty percent, so eventually some of them have died in the process.

Q. Is it then your opinion if these embryos are left in this frozen condition indefinitely, ultimately they will perish?

A. If they were to be protected for a long time, I would put them in liquid hydrogen, but it will cost very much.

Q. If they're in liquid nitrogen which is not absolute zero, is it your opinion that they would ultimately perish?

A. I cannot tell time but ultimately.

Q. Is it your opinion that the ultimate effect of storage

in cryopreservation ultimately would have the same effect as destroying them now?

A. In the ultimate, yes, but I dislike to speak about very long time because I'm not sure of what would happen in between.

Q. Yes, sir. You indicated that you do not object to in-vitro fertilization as a process, do you?

A. I do not favor it for theoretical reasons. I guess it's a trick we use now in the present stage of knowledge, but it's not the best answer. If you read the newspaper it seems to be the last word about helping reproduction, and I guess it's a wrong idea. But that is a technical opinion.

Q. Even though it may not be the ultimate solution, the ideal solution, you would concede that many, many infertile couples have been helped by in-vitro fertilization, would you not?

A. I would consider some have been helped, but the number that have been helped by other methods is much greater. But some have been helped, no doubt.

Q. Doctor, you indicated that one of the reasons you objected to cryopreservation was because there is a mortality rate, certain percentage of the embryo do not survive the process, is that correct?

A. It's not only that. That is one of the reasons, but it's not the only reason.

Q. Are you aware, Doctor, in a normal cycle, a natural reproductive cycle that as many as sixty percent of the ova produced by a mother undergo actual fertilization? Are you familiar with that particular statistic?

A. No, I don't understand what you mean.

Q. We have been told that as many as sixty percent of the eggs produced by a mother may be actually fertilized, but statistically only about twenty-five actually result in a birth.

A. You mean about the early death of early human beings. Well, it has been a very disputed field. To the best of our knowledge, we can rely on experimental animals because we can look at the number of yellow corpus which develops on the ovary and tells us how many eggs have been laid and look at the litter, for example, in mice or any other animals. It seems that thirty percent of the *conceptus* die, but that more than sixty percent of *conceptus* come to birth and to normal—that has been established in many wild animals. Then it seems that the number of early deaths has been overestimated recently in our species. I would guess it around the order of thirty percent. Some of them said sixty percent; I would guess myself it's around closer to thirty than to sixty, but that is —

Q. You do recognize —

A. A sizable number.

Q. You do recognize, do you not, though, Doctor, that when a man and woman attempt to have a child by normal sexual intercourse, there is a percent of embryo human beings, in your terminology, that are created that never result in a birth; that is a risk they undergo?

A. It's difficult to answer your question because some of those fertilizations are probably abnormal fertilizations that can be early cysts and what we call empty cysts which are probably not really true fertilizations. It is very complex, but I agree with you that the road of life is dangerous, even at the very beginning.

Q. I guess my question is, Doctor, then even in natural

intercourse trying to achieve a pregnancy, there are going to be some risks that some of the embryo will not survive, just like in-vitro fertilization?

A. Yeah.

Q. Finally, Doctor, as I understand your testimony here today, if you were advising his Honor on a solution to this very troublesome problem, your first preference would be that the embryo be returned to the mother, Mrs. Davis, in this case, is that correct?

A. I would go step by step, if you ask me. May I, your Honor?

THE COURT: Yes, you may.

THE WITNESS: I would first say it's not a property so they must not be destroyed. Secondly, they have been put into suspended time in the hope that some day they will be given shelter by their own mother, and their mother offers them shelter. I don't see any reason not to grant it to them and to her.

Q. Let me take that one step further: if his Honor should decide for some reason that it is not appropriate that Mrs. Davis, the mother, should have these embryo, would you then agree that the second preference, the second best solution would be to donate them to some other couple, some other mother who would bring them into being, or attempt to bring them into being?

A. I would agree with that because that would preserve the life of the embryos, but then if you agree with that, you are coming back to the Solomon decision. The true mother is the one who prefer the baby given to another than the baby being killed. Then I would suppose that the justice would be on the side of Solomon.

MR. TAYLOR: We all hope his Honor has the wisdom of Solomon. Thank you, Doctor.

THE COURT: Do you have anything?

MR. CHRISTENBERRY: No, thank you, your Honor.

THE COURT: Any recross?

MR. CLIFFORD: No, your Honor.

THE COURT: Dr. Lejeune, you may come down and have a seat over here with Mr. Palmer and Mr. Christenberry.

(The witness was excused.)

Pro-Life Resources

There are a large number of pro-life organizations that can provide you with further information about the abortion debate. The following list is by no means comprehensive, but it should give you a good start.

American Center for Law
and Justice
P.O. Box 90555
Washington, DC 20090-0555
www.aclj.org

American Family Association
P.O. Box 2440
Tupelo, MS 38803
www.afa.net

American Life League
P.O. Box 1350
Stafford, VA 22555
www.all.org

Birthright International
P.O. Box 98363
Atlanta, GA 30359-2063
www.birthright.org

Care Net
44180 Riverside Parkway
Suite 200
Lansdowne, VA 20176
www.care-net.org

Churches for Life
P.O. Box 411752
St. Louis, MO 63141
www.getintolife.org

Concerned Women for America
   1015 Fifteenth St. NW
   Suite 1100
   Washington, D.C. 20005
   www.cwfa.org

Conservative Caucus
   450 Maple Ave. East
   Vienna, VA 22180
   www.conservativeusa.org

Coral Ridge Ministries
   P.O. Box 1920
   Ft. Lauderdale, FL 33302
   www.coralridge.org

Eagle Forum
   P.O. Box 618
   Alton, IL 62002
   www.eagleforum.org

Eternal Perspective Ministries
   39085 Pioneer Blvd., Suite 206
   Sandy, OR 97055
   www.epm.org

Family Research Council
   801 G St. NW
   Washington, D.C. 20001
   www.frc.org

Focus on the Family
   Colorado Springs, CO 80995
   www.focusonthefamily.com

40 Days for Life
   3515-B Longmire #316
   College Station, TX 77845
   www.40daysforlife.com

Human Life International
   4 Family Life Lane
   Front Royal, VA 22630
   www.hli.org

King's Meadow Study Center
   P.O. Box 1601
   Franklin, TN 37065
   www.kingsmeadow.com

Life Decisions International
   P.O. Box 439
   Front Royal, VA 22630-0009
   www.fightpp.org

Life Dynamics
   204 Cardinal Drive
   Denton, TX 76209
   www.lifedynamics.com

Life Issues Institute
1821 W. Galbraith Road
Cincinnati, OH 45239
www.lifeissues.org

National Institute of Family
and Life Advocates
P.O. Box 42060
Fredericksburg, VA 22404
www.nifla.org

National Right to Life
Committee
512 Tenth St. NW
Washington, DC 20004
www.nrlc.org

Pro-Life Action League
6160 N. Cicero Ave.
Chicago, IL 60646
www.prolifeaction.org

Stop Planned Parenthood
International
P.O. Box 1350
Stafford, VA 22555
www.stopp.org

World Magazine
P.O. Box 20002
Asheville, NC 28802
www.worldmag.com

Notes

1   Planned Parenthood Federation of America, "2008 Service Report," 2–4.

2   *Planned Parenthood Insider*, April 1993.

3   PPFA, "Service Report," 19–24.

4   *Planned Parenthood Insider*, July-August 1993.

5   Ibid.; cf. *National STOPP News*, Nov. 30, 1993.

6   Planned Parenthood Federation of America, "2008 Annual Report," 21.

7   Madeline Gray, *Margaret Sanger: A Biography* (New York: Marek, 1979), 326.

8   PPFA, "Service Report," 21.

9   Ibid.

10 Ibid.; cf. International Planned Parenthood Federation, "2002 Annual Report," 22; *National STOPP News*, Nov. 30, 1993.

11 *LifeNews*, Dec. 20, 2009 (http://www.lifenews.com/obamaabortionrecord.html).

12 *National Catholic Register*, March 28, 2009 (http://www.ncregister.com/daily/obama_100_days_of_abortion).

13 Gallup Poll, May 15, 2009 (www.gallup.com/poll/118399/More-Americans-Pro-Life-Than-Pro-Choice-First-Time.aspx).

14 The Pew Research Center, October 2009 (http://people-press.org/report/549/support-for-abortion-slips).

15 Rasmussen Poll, May 26, 2009.

16 G. T. Burkman, et al., "Culture and Treatment Results in Endometritis Following Elective Abortion," *American Journal of Obstetrics and Gynecology* 128:5; C. Gassner and C. Ballard, "Emergency Medicine after Abortion Abscess," *American Journal of Obstetrics and Gynecology*, 128:4; D. Trichopoulos, et al., "Induced Abortion and Secondary Infertility," *British Journal OB/GYN* 83;

K. A. Stallworthy, et al., "Legal Abortion: A Critical Assessment of its Risks," *The Lancet*, 12:4; American Association of Blood Banks and The American Red Cross, "Circular Information," 1984, 6; W. Cates, et al., "Thromboembolism and Abortion," *American Journal of Obstetrics and Gynecology* 132:4; R. L. Turner, *Complications and Consequences of Abortion* (Los Angeles: Advocates for Life Press, 1983), 4; L. Duenhoelter and B. Grant, "Complications Following Prostaglandin F-2A Induced Mid-trimester Abortion," *American Journal of Obstetrics and Gynecology*, 146:2.

17 *Health Care Reform Gazetteer*, November 2009; cf. *Omni Magazine*, October 1991; Julia Wittleson, *The Feminization of Poverty* (Boston: Holy Cross Press, 1983), 122–125. Direct causality is difficult to prove, of course, but no other single factor has so affected the health-care world to separate men and women more than gynecological innovations such as abortion. Even the changing shape of the workforce to include more women has been neutralized as a factor in costs by group health insurance stabilization.

18 Planned Parenthood Federation of America, "A Risky Business: Reproductive Health Care in Litigation," 1998.

19 *New York Times*, June 19, 1993.

20 Scott Somerville, ed., *The Link Between Abortion and Breast Cancer* (Purcellville, Va.: AIM, 1993).

21 *The St. Louis Wire*, Spring 2004.

22 *National Right to Life News*, June 15, 1995.

23 Ibid.

24 *Hong Kong Eastern Express*, April 12, 1995.

25 *New Dimensions*, October 1991.

26 *Austin American-Statesman*, Nov. 22, 1993.

27 *National Institute of Family and Life Advocates Legal Update*, July-August 2007.

28 Front Lines Research, November 2000.

29 *Caveat Journal*, Nov. 2, 2009.

30 *Health Care Reform Gazetteer*, November 2009.

31 George Grant, *Grand Illusions: The Legacy of Planned Parenthood* (Franklin, Tenn.: King's Meadow, 1988, 1992, 2010).

32 For the story of this remarkable pro-life resurgence, see George Grant, *Third Time Around: The History of the Pro-Life Movement from the First Century to the Present* (Franklin, Tenn.: King's Meadow, 1990, 2010); and Marvin Olasky, *The*

Press and Abortion, 1838–1988 (Hillsdale, N.J.: Lawrence Erlbaum Associates, Publishers, 1988).

33 See James Macaulay, *Current Heroes: Examples of Faith for Our Time* (New York: American Tract Society, 1879), 56–57; James C. Mohr, *Abortion in America: The Origins and Evolution of National Policy* (New York: Oxford University Press, 1978), 221–224; E. Frank Howe, *Sermon on Ante-Natal Infanticide* (Terra Haute, Ind.: Allen & Andrews, 1869), 2; Minutes of the General Assembly of the Presbyterian Church in the United States of America, XVIII (Philadelphia: Presbyterian Publications Committee, 1869), 937.

34 Winston C. Duke and Paul Fowler, *Abortion: Toward an Evangelical Consensus* (Portland, Ore.: Multnomah, 1987), 36.

35 Edward J. Carnell, *An Introduction to Christian Apologetics* (Grand Rapids: Eerdmans, 1948), 22.

36 See Grant, *Third Time Around.*

37 Michael J. Gorman, *Abortion and the Early Church* (Downers Grove, Ill.: Inter-Varsity, 1982), 21.

38 Ibid., 20.

39 *Early Christian Fathers*, eds. John Baillie, John T. McNeill, and Henry P. Van Dusen, Library of Christian Classics, vol. I (Philadelphia: Westminster, 1953), 172.

40 Ibid., 171.

41 Gorman, *Abortion and the Early Church*, 49.

42 John M. Frame, *Medical Ethics* (Phillipsburg, N.J.: P&R, 1988), 94.

43 Ibid., 99–101. The term *yeled* in Exodus 21:22 is never used to describe a nonviable fetus. The Hebrew language has such a word, *golem*. Used in Psalm 139:16, *golem* literally means "embryo" or "fetus." When Scripture speaks of the death of an unborn child (Job 3:16; Ps. 58:8; Eccl. 6:3), the word is neither *golem* nor *yeled*, but *nefel*, which means "one untimely born." *Yeled*, then, in the absence of strong considerations to the contrary, does not mean a miscarried child. Dr. Frame also examines the verb *yatza*, found in Exodus 21:22. The term means "go out" or "depart." *Yatza* is normally used to describe ordinary births (Gen. 25:26; 38:28–30; Job 10:18; Jer. 1:5; 20:18). The only possible exception is the use of *yatza* in Numbers 12:12. Again, the Hebrew has a more accurate term for miscarriage and spontaneous abortion: *shakol* (Gen. 31:38; Ex. 23:26; Job 2:10; Hos. 9:14; Mal. 3:11). The proper interpretation, then, of the phrase *weyatze'u yeladheyha* in Exodus 21:22 would not be an induced miscarriage nor the death

of an unborn child, but an induced premature birth of a living child. Finally, Dr. Frame examines the term *ason* ("harm") in verses 22 and 23. Had the writer intended to refer only to the woman, *lah* meaning "to her" would have been added. The harm then refers to the woman, to her prematurely born child, or to both. Pro-abortion activists are on shaky ground with this text, whether the broad or narrow interpretation is used.

44 Terry Bosgra, *Abortion, the Bible, and the Church* (Toronto: LifeCycle Books, 1987), 7–8.

45 Cited in John Jefferson Davis, *Evangelical Ethics* (Phillipsburg, N.J.: P&R, 1985), 134.

46 Cited in Robert H. Bork, *The Tempting of America* (New York: The Free Press, 1990), 14.

47 Ibid.

48 Cited in ibid., 115.

49 Roland Bainton, *Here I Stand: A Life of Martin Luther* (Nashville: Abingdon Press, 1978), 144.

50 Cited in Bork, *The Tempting of America*, 114.

51 Cited in Joseph Wambaugh, *The Blooding* (New York: Bantam Books, 1989), 94.

52 Cited in Bosgra, *Abortion, the Bible, and the Church*, 14.

53 *New York Times*, January 8, 1990, B8.

54 Cited in Charles Colson, *Kingdoms in Conflict* (Grand Rapids: Zondervan, 1987), 101.

55 Ibid., 105.

56 Ibid., 108.

57 Ibid., 125.

58 *New York Times*, January 8, 1990, A1, B8.

Bibliography

Alcorn, Randy. *Pro-Life Answers to Pro-Choice Questions*. Portland, Ore: Multnomah, 1992, 2000.

Bajema, Clifford E. *Abortion and the Meaning of Personhood*. Grand Rapids: Baker, 1974.

Belz, Mark. *Suffer the Little Children*. Wheaton, Ill.: Crossway, 1989.

Brown, Harold O. J. *Death Before Birth*. Nashville: Thomas Nelson, 1977.

Fowler, Paul B. *Abortion—Toward an Evangelical Consensus*. Portland, Ore.: Multnomah, 1987.

Ganz, Richard L. *Thou Shalt Not Kill*. New Rochelle, N.Y.: Arlington House, 1978.

Grant, George. *Grand Illusions—The Legacy of Planned Parenthood*. Franklin, Tenn.: King's Meadow, 1988, 2000, 2010.

_____. *Third Time Around: The History of the Pro-Life Movement from the First Century to the Present*. Franklin, Tenn.: King's Meadow, 1990, 2010.

_____. *Killer Angel: The Life and Legacy of Margaret Sanger*. Franklin, Tenn.: King's Meadow, 1994, 2000, 2010.

Klasen, Thomas G. *A Pro-Life Manifesto*. Wheaton, Ill.: Crossway, 1988.

Montgomery, John Warwick. *Slaughter of the Innocents*. Wheaton, Ill.: Crossway, 1981.

Olasky, Marvin. *The Press and Abortion, 1838–1988*. Hillsdale, N.J.: Lawrence Erlbaum Associates, 1988.

Reardon, David C. *Aborted Women—Silent No More*. Wheaton, Ill.: Crossway, 1987.

Schaeffer, Francis A., and C. Everett Koop. *Whatever Happened to the Human Race?* Old Tappan, N.J.: Fleming H. Revell, 1979.

Young, Curt. *The Least of These*. Chicago: Moody Press, 1984.

Index

About the Author

Dr. R. C. Sproul is the founder and chairman of Ligonier Ministries, an international multimedia ministry based in Lake Mary, Florida. He also serves as senior minister of preaching and teaching at Saint Andrew's in Sanford, Florida, and as chancellor of the Ligonier Academy of Biblical and Theological Studies, and his teaching can be heard around the world on the daily radio program *Renewing Your Mind*.

During his distinguished academic career, Dr. Sproul helped train men for the ministry as a professor at several leading theological seminaries.

He is the author of more than seventy books, including *The Holiness of God*, *Chosen by God*, *The Invisible Hand*, *Faith Alone*, *A Taste of Heaven*, *Truths We Confess*, *The Truth of the Cross*, and *The Prayer of the Lord*. He also served as general editor of *The Reformation Study Bible* and has written several children's books, including *The Prince's Poison Cup*.

Dr. Sproul and his wife, Vesta, make their home in Longwood, Florida.